PRAISE FOR *Sweet Eats for All*

"Anyone who loves desserts, whether or not they have dietary restrictions, will be delighted by the dazzling collection of irresistible recipes. From cakes, to cookies, candies (lollipops!), ice cream, even puff pastry—every category of sweet treats is represented. Lots of photographs, tips, techniques, conversions and substitutions, make this book as useful as it tempting!"—**Fran Costigan**, author of *Vegan Chocolate* and *More Great Good Dairy Free Desserts Naturally*

"Gluten-free guru Allyson Kramer does it again—this time, with a dazzling collection of sumptuous recipes for all manner of cakes, cookies, pies, and more (including puff pastry!) that are both gluten-free and vegan."—**Robin Robertson**, bestselling author of *Vegan Without Borders*, *Vegan Planet*, *Quick-Fix Vegan*, and many more

"As a dietitian who recommends a wholesome, health-promoting diet, I would be remiss if I didn't promote occasional decadent deliciousness. From homemade staples to cakes, cookies, ice cream, and more, *Sweet Eats for All* is sweet vegan, gluten-free heaven!"—**Julieanna Hever, MS, RD, CPT**, author of *The Complete Idiot's Guide to Plant-Based Nutrition* and *The Vegiterranean Diet*

"Allyson takes you from Almond Bon Bons to White Chocolate Peanut Butter Pretzel Tartlets and leaves nothing out in between. This is the new go-to allergy friendly cookbook for a sweet tooth. She brings cakes, cookies, pies, pastries, ice cream, puddings, candy and more back into your life. This book even has my new favorite dessert— Butternut Pots de Creme topped with smoked salt!"—**Kathy Hester**, author of *OATrageous Oatmeals* and *The Great Vegan Bean Book*

"In these pages, you'll find desserts that are free of common allergens, 100% vegan, and also totally satisfying. Kramer evokes beloved childhood while also keeping an eye on whole food ingredients. This is the ultimate collection for dessert lovers who happen to enjoy eating (and sharing) healthful, innovative plant-based food." —**Gena Hamshaw, C.C.N.**, author of *Choosing Raw*

PRAISE FOR *Great Gluten-Free Vegan Eats*

"Blogger Allyson Kramer does what many thought impossible: she makes tasty, delicious food that is gluten-free. Simply put, this book wooed a staff that, shall I say, hasn't always fully embraced foods made sans wheat protein. Kramer packs a winning one-two combo: she is a gluten-free flour expert, and she knows how to use them. You won't miss a thing."—**Joseph Connelly**, Publisher, *VegNews Magazine*

"Allyson Kramer's debut cookbook is the essential guide for deliciously creative, gluten-free, vegan eats! Filled with gorgeous photographs and mouthwatering recipes like Banana Berry Cobbler and Spinach Artichoke Dip, *Great Gluten-Free Vegan Eats* will inspire you to cook in a whole new way!"—**Julie Hasson**, author of *Vegan Diner*

"It takes a lot of talent to adhere to two dietary restrictions and still come out with tasty recipes the way Allyson Kramer has done in *Great Gluten-Free Vegan Eats*."—***Vegetarian Times***

"*Great Gluten-Free Vegan Eats* is a solid reflection of Allyson Kramer's style and a shining example of why her blog, Manifest Vegan, has become so popular. Allyson delights the senses with stunning visuals, flavorful ingredients, and simplistic recipes that will make you forget about eggs, dairy, and gluten altogether."—**Alisa Fleming, author of *Go Dairy Free: The Guide and Cookbook***

"Being a gluten-free vegan just got a whole lot better, thanks to Allyson Kramer. In *Great Gluten-Free Vegan Eats*, Allyson dishes up a broad range of creative, tasty dishes. With beautiful photographs, this book will tempt eaters of all dietary persuasions."—**Tamasin Noyes, author of *American Vegan Kitchen***

"Allyson's recipes are living proof that vegan as well as gluten-free food is delicious and fun! 'You can eat cake' . . . and then some!"—**Carolyn Scott-Hamilton, author of *The Healthy Voyager's Global Kitchen***

Naturally Lean

Naturally Lean

125 Nourishing Gluten-Free,
Plant-Based Recipes—
ALL UNDER 300 CALORIES

ALLYSON KRAMER

Da Capo
LIFE
LONG

A Member of the Perseus Books Group

Designed by Megan Jones Design, www.meganjonesdesign.com
Set in 10.75 point Archer Book by Megan Jones Design

Cataloging-in-Publication data for this book is available from the Library of Congress.

First Da Capo Press edition 2016

Paperback ISBN: 978-0-7382-1856-4
Ebook ISBN: 978-0-7382-1857-1

Published by Da Capo Press
A Member of the Perseus Books Group
www.dacapopress.com

Note: The information in this book is true and complete to the best of our knowledge. This book is intended only as an informative guide for those wishing to know more about health issues. In no way is this book intended to replace, countermand, or conflict with the advice given to you by your own physician. The ultimate decision concerning care should be made between you and your doctor. We strongly recommend you follow his or her advice. Information in this book is general and is offered with no guarantees on the part of the authors or Da Capo Press. The authors and publisher disclaim all liability in connection with the use of this book.

Da Capo Press books are available at special discounts for bulk purchases in the U.S. by corporations, institutions, and other organizations. For more information, please contact the Special Markets Department at the Perseus Books Group, 2300 Chestnut Street, Suite 200, Philadelphia, PA 19103, or call (800) 810-4145, ext. 5000, or e-mail special. markets@perseusbooks.com.

10 9 8 7 6 5 4 3 2

For my two beautiful children,
Landen and Olive.

CONTENTS

1   INTRODUCTION

4   Eating Naturally Lean

5   Healthy Happy Tips for Living the
    Naturally Lean Way

7   Good-for-You Ingredients Guide

13 Helpful Tools and Gadgets

CHAPTER 1
GREENS & CRUCIFERS

19 Serious Taco Salad

20 Mighty Mac and Collards

21 Curried Collard Wraps

22 Korean Napa Tacos

23 Wakame Salad

24 Easy Kimchi

27 Power Up Kale Salad

28 Red Potato Watercress Salad

31 Garlicky Rainbow Chard and Cannellinis

32 Apple-Infused Shredded Brussels

33 Almond-Roasted Romanesco

34 Oil-Free Roasted Broccoli

35 Sweet Mustard–Glazed Rapini

36 Spinach Artichoke Dip

39 Cheesy BBQ Kale Chips

40 Strawberry Banana Green Smoothie

42 Mint Chocolate Chip Smoothie

43 Walnut Arugula Pesto

44 Greenest Goddess Dressing

CHAPTER 2
HEARTY GRAINS

47 Three-Grain Breakfast Medley

48 Goji Overnight Oats

50 Choco-Chip, PB, & Banana Oatmeal
    (a.k.a. My Favorite Oatmeal)

51 Not-So-Dirty Rice

53 Wild Rice Pilaf

54 Red Quinoa Tabbouleh

57 Summertime Quinoa Bowl

58 Get Up and Go Granola

60 Blackberry Coconut Quinoa

61 Cherry Almond Millet

62 Chocolate Teff Waffles

63 Cinnamon Pumpkin Donuts

65 Cinnamon Bun Milk Shake

66 Banana Oatmeal Raisin Cookies

69 Chocolate Brownie Cake

70 Oh-So-Rich Chocolate Glaze

CHAPTER 3
FABULOUS FRUITS

72 Light and Lemony Fusilli with Asparagus and Roasted Tomatoes

75 Roasted Grape and Asparagus Salad

76 Dilly Avocado Toasts

79 Kabocha, Apple, and Fennel Bisque

80 Creamy Tomato Bisque

81 Plantain Tacos

82 Sun-Dried Tomato Guacamole

83 Superfresh Salsa

84 Papaya Salad

85 Minted Watermelon Salad

86 Kiwi Salad

87 Dried Fruit Salad

88 Lemony Lime Chia Pudding

91 Carrot Applesauce Muffins

92 Easy as Sunday Morning Banana Pancakes

93 Cinnamon Plum Streusel

94 Roasted Pears with Walnuts

95 Chocolate Gooseberry Pudding

96 Caramel Apple Parfaits

97 Hunky Monkey Ice Cream

98 Blueberries and Cream Mousse

99 Cantaloupe Mango Sorbet

100 Cardamom Orange Ice

101 Beyond Good BBQ Sauce

102 Raspberry Vinaigrette

105 ACV Fizz

106 Rosemary Cucumber Cooler

CHAPTER 4
NUTS & SEEDS

111 Insanely Addictive Queso

112 Pad Thai Soba Noodles

113 Thai Peanut Dressing

114 Pecan-Stuffed Okra

115 Walnut Eggplant Dip

116 Flax and Chia Garlic Crackers

117 Simple Soft and Chewy Granola Bars

118 Chewy Cherry Chia Bars

119 Cocoa Carob Bars

120 Vanilla Almond Granola

123 Nutty Butter Cookies

124 Chocolate-Covered Hemp Cookies

125 Caramel Pepita Cookies

126 Chocolate Cheesecake

127 Chocolate Gelato

128 Too Good for You to Be True Chocolate

129 Chocolate Hazelnut Bites

130 White Chocolate Peanut Butter Fudge Bites

133 Cashew Milk

134 Almond Milk

135 Simple Cashew Cream

136 Creamy Cashew Cheese

137 Brazil Nut Ricotta

138 Parmesan Sprinkles

139 Stealthy Healthy Mayo

CHAPTER 5
LEGUMES

142   Crispy Baked Falafel

145   Popcorn Tofu

146   Avocado Chick'n Salad

147   Rainbow Veggie Chili

148   Zesty Black Bean Soup

149   Roasted Corn and Cilantro Chili

150   Sunshine Breakfast UnScramble

152   Red Bean Sweet Potato Salad

153   Orange Lentil Salad

155   Tempeh and Snow Peas

156   Pesto Haricots Verts

157   Oil-Free Hummus

158   Pizza Hummus

159   Peanut Butter Black Bean Brownie Bites

160   Lighten Up Pizza Crust

161   White Bean Ranch Dressing

CHAPTER 6
SQUASH, ROOTS, & MUSHROOMS

164   Yukon-Stuffed Poblanos

167   Zucchini-Laced Fusilli

168   Magnificent Mushroom Pizza

170   Rustic Ratatouille

171   Super Easy Veggie Broth

173   Spaghetti Squash with Broccoli and Button Mushrooms

174   Brilliant Beet Soup

175   Sweet Potato Cauliflower Soup

176   Cream of Shiitake Soup

179   Carrot Rutabaga Butternut Bisque

180   Cheesy Potato Soup

181   Portobello Bacon

182   New Potato Poppers

183   Delicata Squash Millet Bowl

184   Ricotta-Stuffed Creminis

187   Cucumber, Mango, and Radish Salad

188   Roasted Radishes and Yellow Beets

191   Cheesy Chili Sweet Potato Fries

192   Glazed Baby Carrots

195   Ravishing Red Slaw

196   Jicama and Beet Green Frittata

197   Carrot Cake Smoothie

198   Half and Half Marinara Sauce

199   RECIPE PAIRING SUGGESTIONS

201   METRIC CONVERSIONS

202   ACKNOWLEDGMENTS

203   ABOUT THE AUTHOR

204   INDEX

INTRODUCTION

For as long as I can remember I have been passionate about food. But, for many years, I also struggled with my weight and accepting my body—and I'm guessing that some of you can relate to my experience. I grew up in the 1980s and '90s, when convenience trumped health in most food situations. Fast food was commonplace on our dinner table, as were all sorts of prepackaged meals filled with empty calories and hydrogenated fats. Comfort food was then the bulk of my diet and I never thought twice about it: it tasted great, was easy

to obtain, and everyone else was eating that way. As I grew into my teens, I realized that I couldn't maintain a healthy weight on these junk and comfort foods, and I found myself turning to food restriction and dieting more often than I'd like to admit.

At the age of only fourteen, I thought that the key to a happy, healthy life was mastering the art of eating less. With this line of thinking, I found myself on a downward spiral. For almost fifteen years I had disordered eating habits that had a negative impact on my health and made food the focus of my life. I yo-yoed between weight gain and weight loss, and it did a whopper on my self-esteem.

Over time I ended up making food my enemy, even though it was something that brought joy to my life. Out of curiosity and desperation to end this vicious cycle, I started searching for some healthier ways to enjoy foods. This led me to discover new fruits, vegetables, and grains, and I was fascinated to learn how they impacted our body. I hadn't realized how the types of food we consume directly affect our mental and physical health.

This was a breakthrough in my thinking and I haven't viewed food the same since. We've all heard the adage "You are what you eat." While it's a very simplified way to express a quite complex idea, it couldn't be truer. Whole foods—foods that are minimally processed, such as fruits, vegetables, beans, grains, greens, and seeds—support a healthy lifestyle, from weight management to healthy aging, and there are so many reasons to make sure you're eating them in abundance and limiting your intake of processed foods. By eating more whole foods, you are consuming lower-calorie choices that are packed full of nutrients that will make your mind and body stronger, more energetic, and simply healthier. Because you aren't filling your body with empty calories and simple sugars, you can eat more, too. The more whole foods you consume, the better you feel.

Our body is designed to utilize nutrients (proteins, carbohydrates, fat, vitamins, and minerals that are essential to our well-being) as well as phytonutrients (plant compounds that aren't essential but help protect against diseases and illness). These nutrients and phytonutrients are found readily within whole foods, and eating a diet mostly composed of whole foods is the most efficient way of delivering nutrients to your body's cells. A plant-based diet is an easy way to introduce more whole foods to your diet. And, by also reducing your intake of gluten, you will rely less on common filler foods, such as bread made with refined white flour, seitan, and highly processed vegan treats, and instead lean toward nutrient-dense foods. Fruits, vegetables, and grains are extremely low in empty calories and high in both insoluble fiber—the kind that helps foods move along our digestive tracts with ease by passing straight through, and soluble fiber—the kind that dissolves in water and binds to other foods slowing digestion that encourages nutrient absorption and keeps you feeling fuller longer.

Whole foods are not only better for you—they are essential. We should choose foods that exist in a fairly natural state over highly processed foods whenever possible; truly they should compose the bulk of our diet. On that note, I do not recommend deprivation and believe that mindful moderation is key. Eat healthy all week, and then have a killer dessert if you'd like on Friday—you get the idea. It's very easy to get off track with trying to be "too pure" in eating, and I would never ever advocate that.

Keep it simple. Seek out foods that are full of nutrients over more processed foods that are "empty" or devoid of any nutritional value. For those who are new to this type of eating, choosing the right foods can be difficult without any know-how. That's where this book comes in! Each recipe within this book is gluten-free, vegan, and made from 100 percent whole food ingredients, and is just as flavorful as any food that is laden with unhealthy and overprocessed ingredients. By readers' request, I've also included an "oil free" **OF** designation on appropriate recipes,

WHAT ABOUT SUPPLEMENTS?

Even though we can get some of the nutrients found in whole foods in the form of vitamin and mineral supplements, evidence from recent studies suggest that they simply won't be absorbed as well as they would from whole foods. Manufacturers and distributors do not need FDA approval to sell dietary supplements, and the labels on these supplements may make claims about nutritional values that are not entirely accurate.

The FDA does not analyze supplements prior to their being sold to consumers, so you may even be taking a gamble on your health by relying on supplements to fulfill your nutritional needs. However, taking supplements in addition to a balanced diet containing whole foods is certainly an option for many individuals and a topic to discuss with your physician or nutritionist. In fact, vegans should supplement their diet with vitamin B12, as this nutrient is quite difficult to obtain through a 100 percent plant-based diet.

However, if you only get your nutrients from supplementation, you are still going to need food to satiate your hunger. Supplementation can trick us into thinking it's okay to indulge in multiple servings of processed or shelf-stable prepackaged meals throughout the day (since we already consumed needed nutrients in the supplements). Yet, we are depriving our body of easy nourishment from whole foods and instead relying on a magic pill that may not even work that well. Highly processed, or "filler," foods satiate our hunger quickly and then turn to fat stores on our body unless we are burning the calories as fast as we consume them. And even if we are burning enough calories while subsisting on these foods, our cells are having a hard time keeping up without the proper nourishment.

so that people who eat little to no oil (often following the dietary advice of Dr. Caldwell B. Esselstyn, Dr. John McDougall, and/or Dr. Joel Fuhrman) can also enjoy many of these recipes with ease. I want to show you the variety of plants that are ready to be enjoyed—how to prepare them, how to incorporate them into your daily life, and how to love them. I am not a health professional—I'm simply sharing what works best for me after years of struggling to find something, anything that

would keep me feeling my best both mentally and physically. I still enjoy sugary sweets and other traditional comfort foods from time to time, but these are no longer the majority of my diet. Fresh fruits, colorful veggies, hearty grains, nuts and seeds are just too darn tantalizing to abandon, and I plan to keep them as the main part of how I eat for what I hope to be the rest of my long, healthy life. By eating this way and nourishing my body, I've noticed a positive change in my relationship with food: I'm now able to maintain a healthy weight with little effort. My mental outlook is brighter, my skin is clearer (I used to struggle with cystic acne, yet when I'm eating right, my skin is super clear!), my nails and hair are stronger, and my energy levels stay steady throughout the day (no more three p.m. crashes!). Along with regular exercise, eating nourishing food is the perfect remedy to beating the body blues.

Now, you may find getting plenty of whole foods into your diet easy. You may wake up each morning and enjoy a wholesome breakfast and large glass of water and get plenty of fresh fruits and vegetables throughout the day. If this is you, you are awesome and your body knows it. Keep it up! And, read on for some more whole foods inspiration. If it's not you (you are awesome, too!), use the recipes on the following pages to help you make more colorful and nutritious choices.

For example, if you eat fast food three times a day, try replacing just one meal with one made from a colorful array of whole foods, such as a giant salad or my Curried Collard Wraps (page 21). Adding more whole foods to your daily diet will make a huge impact on your health and most likely will prompt you to make healthier choices more often—hopefully to the point where you will be enjoying fast food only on occasion.

EATING NATURALLY LEAN

I want to stress that this book is about eating lean and, more important, mindfully. That simply means cutting out the unpronounceable additives, highly processed ingredients, added sugars, and the like. This book is not about eating less. I solidly back a diet that is not only nutrient dense, but also filling. My motto is, if I'm still hungry . . . eat more! Keep in mind that by "more," I not only mean more food, but also foods that are more nutritious: higher in nutrients and lower in calories than a typical fast-food meal or convenience food. So, if I'm still feeling a bit hungry after a meal or before one, I don't deprive myself; instead I reach for some fresh veggies and guacamole, an apple with nut butter, a banana, a plate of crisp cucumbers with hummus, or another nutritious snack until my hunger is curbed.

There are a lot of small "side dish"–type recipes in this book because I like to create a few small dishes and enjoy them together. It makes for nice harmony of nutrients, taste, and texture, and that makes eating healthier a lot more fun. Many of the smaller recipes included in this book pair marvelously with one another, such as the Curried Collard Wraps and Cheesy Chili Sweet Potato Fries (for more ideas, see recipe pairings and meal suggestions, page 199). Others are hearty and are filling enough as a full meal on their own, such as the Serious Taco Salad or Light and Lemony Fusilli. Eating not only a wide variety of foods, but also *enough* of those foods, is super important to your physical and mental health. Only you know how many calories you need per day, depending on your height, weight, metabolism, and activity level. I recommend making sure you're getting enough—it will ensure that your hunger will stay at bay, which will in turn make it much easier to choose healthy foods, rather than eating whatever is available for a quick calorie fix.

Eating the best foods you can is key. I admit that sometimes that is easier said than done, but the knowledge here is the power. Go ahead and treat yourself every now and again with whatever you'd like to eat, but for the majority of your days, enjoy plenty of nutrient-dense foods and be sure to treat your body with respect. When you eat healthier foods, you provide your entire body, from your hair down to your toes, with the nutrients it needs to thrive.

HEALTHY HAPPY TIPS FOR LIVING THE NATURALLY LEAN WAY

H2Ohh Yea!

One of the best things you can do for yourself if you're not drinking enough water is to start drinking more water. Today. If you're feeling famished, you are probably also a bit dehydrated, so drinking water before, during, and after meals (basically all day long) will help you keep your appetite under control and your energy levels up. On average, healthy women need about 2.2 liters of water per day and men need 3 liters. If you're not close to that number, increase it and watch what it does for your overall glow. You don't need anything fancy; I like to keep a water bottle with me at all times, and I encourage you to do the same. If your office has a water cooler, drink up! If you'd like to drink more at home but don't like the taste of tap water, simply add a splash of lemon or lime juice.

Get Bubbly!

I used to be horribly addicted to diet soda, and water never appealed to me much, even though I knew I should be drinking a lot of it. My solution? Seltzer! It's cheap, and free of added sugars and the phosphoric acid found in sodas. Plus, it's bubbly! I drink about three 16-ounce "sodas" a day, which is just seltzer with a touch of flavor, such as lemon, lime or grapefruit juice.

Salad Stacker

My favorite trick for increasing the nutrient value of almost every meal while adding some bulk with minimal calories: add greens! Simply grab a handful of prepped greens (any will do: baby arugula, chopped kale, Bibb lettuce, collard greens, romaine lettuce, spring mix—you name it) and place it in the bottom of a bowl or deep-dish plate. Then, simply top the greens with whatever you are eating for breakfast, lunch, or dinner. This works so well with pasta dishes (e.g., Mighty Mac and Collards, page 20) or chili (e.g., Rainbow

Veggie Chili, page 147) and well, just about anything. Frittatas, savory grits, Pad Thai Soba Noodles (page 112), are all made a touch tastier and healthier with the simple addition of greens.

If you buy a bunch of greens in bulk, cut down future salad making time by washing, drying, and chopping the greens and then storing them in one of those handy containers that precut greens are packaged in or another breathable container.

Get Moving!

Did you know that even five minutes of running a day can extend your life and decrease your chance for heart disease? Walking is also beneficial and most of us do it quite a bit already—even more reason to try and sneak in extra steps each day. If you hate the word *exercise*, then don't exercise; instead have fun! Go on a hike, have a dance party, take your pup for a long walk, swim a few laps at the pool, ride a bike, or play a game of Frisbee with your pals. As long as you're moving your body and increasing your heart rate, you're exercising!

More Is Better!

If you're having trouble keeping off excess weight, try adding a bit more to your day—meaning more of the fruits and vegetables you love, and more time for treating yourself to exercise. For example, if you are a sucker for tangerines (like I am), then increase how many you eat during the day and indulge in

them over other, less healthy snacks. If you normally walk or run a mile a day, add another quarter-mile to your daily routine. If you often try and snag the closest parking spot, park far away and consider it a fitness blessing in disguise. Just a little increase in healthy eating and exercise can go a long way in your quest for a leaner physique.

GOOD-FOR-YOU INGREDIENTS GUIDE

Before we dive into the recipes, it may be beneficial to get acquainted with a few less common foods that will be mentioned throughout this book. Now that technology has merged with our grocery stores, it's pretty easy to locate any of these foods online (I favor Amazon) or in specialty food stores, but many can also be found at typical chain grocery stores and supermarkets.

Beans

WHERE TO BUY: Supermarkets everywhere

Beans are nutritional powerhouses, boasting a good deal of fiber, protein, and even B vitamins per 1-cup serving. For the recipes where I call for cooked beans, I am referring to either canned beans or cooked dried beans. I prefer to cook my own beans (with less than ¼ teaspoon of salt per pound of beans) for best flavor and texture, but I totally understand the convenience of using canned beans, so I'll leave it up to you in these recipes. The nutritional info given for recipes featuring beans is for cooked and lightly salted beans, so keep in mind the sodium counts will increase if you use salted canned beans.

Chickpea Flour

WHERE TO BUY: Indian groceries, natural food stores, typical grocery chains (in the gluten-free sections), online

This flour, also called garbanzo bean flour, is made from dried ground chickpeas and I love it for its versatility. It works great as a binder, a thickener, a wonderful baking flour, and even an egg replacer, and it adds a bit of protein to your dishes. I recommend seeking out chickpea flour from Indian markets (there called *besan*) for the best flavor and texture, but Bob's Red Mill also has its own variety, which is readily available in many grocery stores. Warning: Don't eat chickpea flour raw! It's not tasty at all when raw, but its flavor is transformed when cooked. Store chickpea flour in a cool, dark area for up to 4 months in an airtight container.

Buckwheat Flour

WHERE TO BUY: Supermarkets, natural food stores, Asian markets, online

Even though this flour's name sounds like it is a relative of wheat and therefore a grass, the buckwheat grains we consume are actually seeds, making it a pseudocereal. It is traditionally enjoyed in many Asian countries where actual wheat may have a hard time growing. Buckwheat flour is a fabulous replacement for traditional wheat flour as it works quite similarly to wheat flour in baked goods and pastas. Buckwheat has an earthy flavor, dark color, and is high in B vitamins, fiber, magnesium, and protein. It also contains a phytochemical called rutin that is known to help strengthen the walls of our already fragile capillaries, which are integral in the exchange of nutrients between our blood and our body's tissues. Store buckwheat flour in an airtight container in a cool, dark spot to best retain freshness, for up to 4 months.

Cacao Butter

WHERE TO BUY: Specialty shops, natural food stores, online

Cacao butter, also called cocoa butter or theobroma oil, is the fat extracted from a cocoa bean that, while in its solid state, resembles a brick (or jar) of solid white chocolate; it melts at body temperature (which is why chocolate melts in your mouth!). Cacao butter is a great source of antioxidants and healthy fatty acids. It is available in many stores, but oftentimes it is sold as an external application, for making body lotions and the like. Be sure to seek out food-grade cacao butter; that way you'll know the quality and taste will be good enough to eat. Store cacao butter in a cool, dry place (I often tuck mine in the fridge door) due to its low melting temperature.

Carob Powder

WHERE TO BUY: Specialty markets, natural food stores, online

A caffeine-free alternative to chocolate, available in flour/powder and chips (the chips have some form of fat added to stabilize). Carob comes from a tree that is found in the Mediterranean. The tree produces pods (legumes) that are dried and then ground into a powder. Carob is naturally sweet, high in protein, low in fat, and delicious! Store carob powder in an airtight container in a dry area.

Chia Seeds

WHERE TO BUY: Supermarkets, natural food stores, online

Chia seeds have made waves in the food world due to their high amounts of omega-3 and -6 fatty acids as well as their ability to fill you up with relatively small serving sizes. Seek out whole chia seeds for puddings or adding to smoothies. To grind, simply pulse a few times in a spice or coffee grinder. Store whole seeds in an airtight container in the pantry for up to 3 months, and store ground seeds in an airtight container in the refrigerator for up to 1 month.

Cocoa Powder

WHERE TO BUY: Supermarkets everywhere and online

Cocoa powder has a deliciously rich flavor; is high in antioxidants, as well as fiber and iron; and is said to have mild antidepressant properties. Cocoa powder is simply ground cocoa beans with most of the fat removed. Cocoa powder comes in a few varieties, such as Dutch-processed, dark, and raw; use any type of cocoa powder you'd like in the recipe that calls for this ingredient. Raw cocoa powder can be found in specialty health food stores and online, but it's not necessary. Even regular and Dutch-processed cocoa have a slew of nutrients and taste delicious. Store cocoa powder in an airtight container.

Coconut Cream

WHERE TO BUY: Supermarkets everywhere and online

Coconut cream can be obtained by refrigerating a can of full-fat coconut milk for about 3 hours and scooping the solid cream that condenses during chilling from the top of the can. (Do not use the coconut cream marketed for use in cocktails because it has added ingredients, such as thickeners and sweeteners.) Feel free to use the remaining coconut milk for other purposes, such as the liquid in baked goods or smoothies. Store unused coconut cream in an airtight container in the refrigerator for up to 3 days.

Dried Goji Berries

WHERE TO BUY: Natural food stores, online

These dried red berries appear in recipes throughout this book. They are actually considered a nightshade, related to eggplants and chile peppers. I jokingly refer to them as nature's fruit snack as they are chewy, tart, tangy, and sweet. These little guys add a burst of fun flavor to so many dishes and they are high in vitamin C and iron. Store for up to 3 months in a tightly sealed resealable plastic bag or airtight container for best taste and texture.

Flaxseed

WHERE TO BUY: Most supermarkets, natural food stores, online

Flaxseed has grown in popularity over the last decade and is touted for its healthy nutritional profile, but I love flaxseed meal simply as a binder or a thickener for a variety of recipes. The fact that flaxseed is high in many minerals, such as copper, iron, magnesium, manganese, and phosphorous, is just a bonus. If you can't locate flaxseed meal, or prefer freshly ground, simply whirl whole flaxseeds in a coffee grinder until powdery. For best taste and freshness, store flaxseeds in an airtight container in the refrigerator for up to 6 months.

Hemp Hearts

WHERE TO BUY: Natural food stores, supermarkets, online

Hemp hearts are the tender, nutty, insides of a shelled hemp seed. They are rapidly gaining popularity among health-foodies due to their mild flavor and impressive nutritional makeup. Hemp hearts boast all nine essential amino acids; are rich in vitamin E, iron, magnesium, phosphorous, and zinc; and are considered a complete protein, making them a smart choice for plant-based eating. Hemp

hearts will usually be located near chia and flaxseeds in your local supermarket or natural food store. Store hemp hearts in your refrigerator in a sealed airtight container to keep fresh for up to 1 year.

Peanut Flour

WHERE TO BUY: Supermarkets, online

Peanut flour is made from peanuts that have been ground, just like peanut butter; yet in peanut flour, the oil is removed after grinding. This flour works great when the familiar flavor of peanut butter is desired, without the added fat or oiliness. Powdered peanut butter also exists, and is usually sold alongside peanut flour—but beware, this stuff often contains added sugars and other ingredients. Seek out flour that has only one ingredient: peanuts. Peanut flour has a good deal of calcium, folate, magnesium, manganese, and protein. Store peanut flour in a cool, dark place in an airtight container for best taste, for up to 4 months.

Raw Cashews

WHERE TO BUY: Chain grocery stores (look in the bulk section), natural food stores, online

Cashews aren't true nuts, but seeds that hang from the bottom of cashew apples, the fruit of the cashew tree. Raw cashews aren't technically raw but steamed, as they would be poisonous to us if we consumed them truly raw; they contain a toxin similar to that of poison ivy. Raw cashews are, however, unroasted and

unsalted. Much paler in color and softer in texture than roasted cashews, these guys work great in so many plant-based applications in place of dairy, which is why I call for them so often throughout the book. I love buying these in bulk through Amazon or other on-line suppliers so I always have plenty on hand for quick sauces, desserts, and creamy bases. Raw cashews are high in copper, magnesium, manganese, and zinc. Store in an airtight container in a cool, dry place.

Silken Tofu

WHERE TO BUY: Most grocery stores, Asian food markets, natural food stores

Mori-Nu is my favorite brand of silken tofu and it comes in a few different varieties that I use throughout this book. It's much softer than regular tofu and can be found on a shelf-stable spot in the supermarket rather than refrigerated. It is available in soft, firm, and extra-firm, as well as light (a.k.a. "lite"), although each variety of silken tofu is, as the name suggests, much silkier and softer than regular tofu. Some people consider tofu, both silken and regular, to be a highly processed food, equivalent to many prepackaged mock meats. While tofu *is* processed, it is only minimally so (it's basically curdled soy milk), and you can easily make your own at home if you desire. Tofu contains minimal ingredients and is much less processed than soy burgers, or even low-fat soy milks, therefore I feel it is closer to a whole food than a processed food.

Tofu is high in calcium, manganese, protein, selenium, zinc, and omega-3 fatty acids.

Sorghum Flour

WHERE TO BUY: Natural food stores, super-markets, online

Sorghum flour comes from the sorghum grass plant, and is one of the first flours I fell in love with after I was diagnosed with celiac disease and had to go gluten-free. Unlike some gluten-free flours, sorghum flour is pale in color and mild in flavor, making it an excellent choice as a nutritious stand-in for wheat flour. Sorghum is high in iron, potassium, thiamine, and protein. Bob's Red Mill brand, which is labeled as "Sweet White Sorghum Flour," is readily found in many supermarkets, often-times alongside other gluten-free flours. I recommend storing sorghum flour in an airtight container in a cool, dark pantry and using within 3 months for best flavor.

Superfine Brown Rice Flour

WHERE TO BUY: Online, specialty stores

This flour is simply brown rice, rich in selenium and fiber, which has been finely ground to give it a silky-smooth texture similar to that of wheat flour. It's my favorite flour for replicating gluten-containing baked goods. If you cannot locate superfine brown rice flour, regular brown rice flour can be substituted, although the texture will be grainier than if superfine is used. Store brown rice flour in an airtight container in a cool, dark place for up to 6 months for best flavor.

Unrefined Sugar

WHERE TO BUY: Natural food stores, supermarkets, online

When I call for unrefined sugar throughout this book, I'm talking about very minimally processed sugars that still retain some nutrient value. Unrefined cane sugar (such as Rapunzel brand), coconut palm sugar, maple sugar, and date sugar all qualify as unrefined sugar. All of these sugars look similar to one another with a deep caramel hue and granular texture, and they can be used fairly interchangeably. Date sugar doesn't dissolve in liquids as the other unrefined sugars—such as coconut palm or maple sugar—do, so it's important to keep that in mind when baking and substituting.

HELPFUL TOOLS AND GADGETS

Here are a few tools that I think are helpful in leading a healthy lifestyle, as they help make cooking effortless. If you have discount stores nearby, such as HomeGoods, Marshalls, or T. J. Maxx, you'll want to check out their selection of kitchen items. They have the best deals on high-quality kitchen gadgets, cookware, and utensils.

APRON: Get one. It will make your life so much easier; and if your clothes stay fresh and clean while you cook, you'll have a much more pleasant experience if you need to do some impromptu cooking when you want a snack.

BAKING SHEETS/PANS: These can be found virtually anywhere that sells kitchen items, from as low as a few dollars apiece. I like to collect several different metal pans in various shapes and sizes so I always have the correct size handy.

BLENDER: I'm not going to deny that high-powered blenders, such as Vitamix and Blendtec, are incredible machines that can completely transform the way you view preparing food, but let's be real—these blenders are pricey, and while lovely, not at all necessary. Any blender should do for the recipes in this book. If you have a Vitamix, great! Use the highest speed for creamy recipes, and shoot for lower speeds on such recipes as the Brazil Nut Ricotta (page 137). If you have a standard blender, it will do just fine.

CANDY MOLDS: These molds, made of silicone or lightweight plastic, can often be found near cake decorating supplies at craft and specialty stores as well as some grocery stores. They make stunning candies with little effort; and at just a few dollars each, they are great to have around for the times you are craving homemade chocolates, such as my Too Good for You to Be True Chocolate (page 128).

CHEESE GRATER: Incredibly handy for quickly shredding carrots, beets, garlic, onion, and practically everything else (be careful—that includes your fingers!). These can be picked up everywhere from drugstores to fancy kitchen supply stores; they're cheap and they last practically forever.

CUTTING BOARD: I'm always amazed at how some people who cook often can go through life without a cutting board. Make your (cooking) life easier and pick one up if you don't already have one. They are so handy and make chopping and slicing vegetables easy and cleanup a breeze. If you only choose one cutting board, I advise getting one that's at least 12 inches long. I prefer plastic as they don't warp as easily as the wooden kinds, but wooden boards are fabulous if you wash and dry them completely after each use and never place them in the dishwasher.

FOOD PROCESSOR: A food processor makes creating cookies, dips, and so much more effortless. You don't need a fancy one; I've found that a simple 7-cup KitchenAid stands up well to a beating (this is my fourth cookbook and mine's still going strong!) and it has replaceable parts, so if your bowl breaks, you're not out completely. The small Cuisinart 3-cup processors are also handy to have around for small batches—for example, halving a recipe, or for quick dips and sauces.

ICE-CREAM MAKER: You can pick up a relatively inexpensive ice-cream maker from just about anywhere these days; I often see the hand-cranked types at many thrift and drugstores. Having used various ice-cream makers for years, I highly recommend investing in a simple electric one. They start at around $50, but I find myself using mine so often, and saving so much money on store-bought ice creams, that it paid itself off in no time. Did I mention that with your own ice-cream maker, you could have delicious, creamy ice cream without any sketchy ingredients any time you'd like? It works so well for dairy-free ice-cream making that I can't imagine my dessert-loving self without one.

KITCHEN KNIVES: You don't need to spend hundreds on a great set of knives to make great-tasting recipes, but sharp and dependable knives are a must for healthy eating. For fresh veggie and fruit chopping, go for a chef's knife or my preference, a Japanese Santoku knife, which has a slightly blunted end and fits better in my smallish hands. I use this knife for slicing and dicing, and if your knife is sharp, you should have excellent precision, enabling you to slice mushrooms and garlic as thin as a mandoline can with a little practice. A dull knife leads to cut-up hands and uncut veggies!

I also find a paring knife ($3 to $20) is handy for peeling and small slicing, zesting, and julienning; and a serrated knife ($5 to $25) is handy for slicing breads and the occasional vegetable in a pinch.

LARGE GLASS JAR: Home goods stores are a great place to pick up one of these jars, which works great for fermenting Easy Kimchi (page 24) and storing homemade nut milks or a batch of cooked dried beans. Make sure that you purchase a good-quality food-grade jar, and it will last you for years and years.

MANDOLINE: A mandoline slicer makes easy work of slicing vegetables in all sorts of shapes, from super thin to crinkle cut, in no time flat. You can find a good-quality mandoline for around $20 at most home goods stores or online. I especially love using a mandoline for recipes that require very thinly sliced ingredients, which can be difficult for even the most savvy knife users. They make perfect cuts every time with no need for any knife skills.

RICE COOKER: This handy little appliance is one that I recommend to anyone who enjoys eating rice and grains. My first rice cooker (in college) saved me so much time and made cooking rice fun! Many models are rather inexpensive and they are a great investment as they make cooking perfect rice totally effortless; just set the appliance, and in 25 to 40 minutes you'll have perfectly cooked rice. Most rice cookers also do well with other grains, such as quinoa, millet, buckwheat, and so much more. My favorite brand of rice cooker is Zojirushi, for both its dependability and ease of use. These can be sourced online and where rice cookers and other small appliances are sold.

SILICONE MAT OR PARCHMENT PAPER: For lower-calorie cooking, either a silicone baking mat or a steady supply of parchment paper is a must for ensuring your recipes don't stick to your pans. If you have these, there is no need for added oil to prevent the sticking, and it makes cleanup so much easier. I tend to prefer silicone mats as they are reusable, but parchment is very handy to have and is less expensive to purchase outright than a mat; although my Silpat mats have lasted through years of baking and cookbook writing, so they are a sound investment.

TOFU PRESS: Tofu presses are a fabulously handy gadget to have around as they save a ton of time and mess when preparing tofu. Probably the most well-known tofu press is the TofuXpress, which I own, love, and highly recommend. It makes pressing tofu effortless and fast, expressing all the water from tofu in only 30 minutes or so. If you don't have a press, you can also press tofu the traditional way: place a block of tofu wrapped snugly in paper towels or a clean kitchen cloth in between two plates. Top the plates with heavy cans or jars (think: canned tomatoes) and wait. Once the paper towels have become drenched with water, change and repeat until all the water is removed. The entire process takes about 3 hours.

CHAPTER 1

GREENS & CRUCIFERS

Greens and crucifers are *the* veggies to be sure you get enough of during the day. But why? What is it that makes greens so extraordinary? Well, first is fiber—the insoluble kind that makes up the bulk of what we know as cellulose. For humans, cellulose is indigestible, but this is a good thing as it helps move all the other stuff along nicely. Greens are also packed with vitamins and minerals and super low on calories. Cruciferous vegetables—such as cauliflower, broccoli, Brussels sprouts, and cabbage—provide the body with glucosinolates, which are thought to help prevent cancer. So, with greens, you get more bang for your nutritional buck.

This section not only covers the wonders of leafy greens, but the cruciferous greens (and their paler cousins) as well.

Serious Taco Salad

Even though this taco salad doesn't call for corn chips, it tastes so much like a taco, you'll never miss those crunchy ol' tortillas. Kale is the star of this salad, packing in a good dose of fiber, antioxidants, and vitamins A, C, and K, while maintaining a low calorie count. It's the perfect green to bulk up a meal without weighing you down.

¾ cup cooked black beans, drained and rinsed

½ teaspoon chili powder

½ teaspoon garlic powder

⅛ teaspoon salt

1 tablespoon minced fresh cilantro

4 heaping cups rinsed, dried, and chopped kale

4 tablespoons Sun-Dried Tomato Guacamole (page 82)

½ cup fresh or frozen corn kernels (thaw if frozen)

½ cup diced and seeded bell pepper

½ cup diced cherry or grape tomatoes

In a small bowl, toss the black beans with the chili powder, garlic powder, and salt and then fold in the cilantro. Place the kale in a separate larger bowl and use clean hands to massage gently with about 4 tablespoons of the Sun-Dried Tomato Guacamole to coat each leaf evenly. Toss with the corn kernels, diced bell pepper, and cherry tomatoes. Top with the seasoned black beans. Enjoy immediately. If you only eat a portion of the salad, store the remaining portion in the refrigerator in an airtight container for up to 2 days.

YIELD:

3 SERVINGS

PER SERVING:

264 CALORIES

3 G FAT

186 MG SODIUM

1,385 MG POTASSIUM

48.9 G CARBOHYDRATES

14 G PROTEIN

This recipe is one of my favorite meals to make after an exhausting day out and about; it really nails the cravings I have for carbs (from the rice pasta), protein, and fat (both thanks to the cashews). It's super creamy and quite cheesy since it features my supertasty queso as its base.

12 ounces brown rice or quinoa penne or macaroni

1 recipe Insanely Addictive Queso (page 111)

1 cup packed chopped collard greens

1 tablespoon water or vegan vegetable broth, such as Super Easy Veggie Broth (page 171)

1 clove garlic, pressed

½ cup finely chopped oil-free sun-dried tomatoes

Freshly ground black pepper

Cook the pasta according to the package directions, and rinse gently in cool water to remove any excess starch. Place the cooked pasta back in the pot and coat evenly with Insanely Addictive Queso sauce.

In a small skillet, toss the collards, the 1 tablespoon of water, pressed garlic, and sun-dried tomatoes together and cook over medium-high heat until the collards are bright and wilted, 1 to 2 minutes. Fold into the pasta and top with black pepper. Serve hot.

Leftovers can be stored in an airtight container for up to 4 days. To reheat, simply place in a shallow pan along with a tablespoon of unsweetened nondairy milk and warm gently until the desired temperature.

YIELD:

8 SERVINGS

PER SERVING:

243 CALORIES

17 G FAT

437 MG SODIUM

539 MG POTASSIUM

18.1 G CARBOHYDRATES

9.3 G PROTEIN

Curried Collard Wraps

No need to break out the bread if you're craving a sandwich; try collard greens to make a satisfying wrap instead. These easy wraps are filled with zesty tempeh salad and are incredibly convenient for lunch if you make them ahead of time and store in aluminum foil for when lunchtime hits.

1 teaspoon olive oil

8 ounces tempeh, any variety

¾ teaspoon salt

1 shallot, finely minced

1 cup diced cucumber

⅔ cup seeded and diced apple

1 teaspoon curry powder

3 tablespoons Stealthy Healthy Mayo (page 139)

1 teaspoon pure maple syrup

6 collard leaves, rinsed and dried, stems removed

In a medium-size skillet, heat the olive oil over medium heat. Crumble the tempeh into bite-size pieces into the pan and lightly sprinkle with ¼ teaspoon of the salt. Toss the tempeh in the pan to brown it on all sides, about 5 minutes. Set aside.

To make the filling, in a medium-size bowl, toss together the shallot, cucumber, apple, remaining ½ teaspoon of salt, and the curry powder. Add the browned tempeh crumbles and stir to combine. Stir in the mayo and maple syrup to thoroughly and evenly coat the tempeh.

Spoon about ½ cup of filling onto each collard leaf, with the filling placed more to one side than the other. Fold the bottom and top of the leaf to envelope the curry mixture, and then roll the leaf up tightly, just like a burrito. These will keep for up to 1 day in an airtight container (aluminum foil or plastic wrap works great to keep them stored snugly) in the refrigerator. Or make the tempeh filling up to 3 days ahead and stuff the collard leaves just before serving.

YIELD:

6 SERVINGS

PER SERVING:

135 CALORIES

7.3 G FAT

318 MG SODIUM

202 MG POTASSIUM

12.3 G CARBOHYDRATES

9.2 G PROTEIN

Korean Napa Tacos

This recipe is a play on the popular food track craze, Korean tacos. These cold tacos use double the napa cabbage: first, napa leaves serve as the taco shell in place of corn tortillas, and then fermented napa, a.k.a. kimchi, is a spicy and crunchy topping.

5 whole leaves napa cabbage (I recommend the bigger, outer leaves)

1 cup walnuts

¼ cup sunflower seeds

1 teaspoon mild taco seasoning (make sure it's wheat/gluten-free, if needed)

1 teaspoon paprika

¼ teaspoon ground coriander

½ teaspoon salt

½ teaspoon ground cumin

1 teaspoon agave or pure maple syrup

⅓ cup Easy Kimchi (page 24) or your favorite brand vegan kimchi

¼ cup shredded carrot

3 tablespoons chopped fresh cilantro

Clean the napa leaves well and slice off the bottom 3 inches or so (the thickest, whitest part) and then fold each napa leaf in half to form a taco shell shape.

Place the walnuts, sunflower seeds, taco seasoning, paprika, coriander, salt, and cumin in a food processor and process until crumbly, about 2 minutes. The mixture should be in fine and even granules, roughly the consistency of cornmeal. Drizzle the agave evenly over the mixture and then pulse a few more times to incorporate throughout.

Divide the filling equally among the five folded leaves and top with kimchi, carrot, and cilantro.

YIELD:

5 SERVINGS

PER SERVING:

153 CALORIES

13.7 G FAT

218 MG SODIUM

189 MG POTASSIUM

4.6 G CARBOHYDRATES

6 G PROTEIN

Wakame Salad

Wakame is a dark green dried sea veggie that can be located at Asian markets or in the Asian food section of many grocery stores. It's flavored with a hint of the sea, with a robust texture that is both filling and refreshing. This salad highlights wakame's unique flavor and satiny texture, which pairs brilliantly with the crisp crunch from cucumber and carrots.

⅓ cup dried wakame

½ cup thinly sliced cucumber

½ cup shelled edamame

3 small carrots, julienned or shredded

1 teaspoon salt or gluten-free soy sauce

3 tablespoons mirin

1 teaspoon pure maple syrup

1 teaspoon sesame oil

1 teaspoon grated fresh ginger

1 clove garlic, pressed or minced

Place the wakame in a medium-size bowl and cover with water. Let rest for 5 to 7 minutes, or until rehydrated. Drain well and rinse with cold water. Transfer the wakame back to the bowl along with the sliced cucumber, edamame, and carrots and toss to combine.

In a small bowl, whisk together the remaining ingredients. Toss evenly with the wakame mixture and let rest for at least 20 minutes before tossing again and then serving.

YIELD:

8 SERVINGS

PER SERVING:

65 CALORIES

1.8 G FAT

497 MG SODIUM

521 MG POTASSIUM

9.9 G CARBOHYDRATES

3.1 G PROTEIN

Easy Kimchi

Crunchy, tangy, healthy kimchi is a delight to have on hand, but can get awfully pricey if you're relying on store-bought. The good news is that it's a cinch to make a home. You just need a few ingredients and three or four days' patience and you'll have more kimchi than you know what to do with. Just kidding; of course, you'll know what to do: eat it every day and bask in its spicy goodness. Korean chili flakes, *gochugaru*, is the main component of kimchi's sweet and smoky flavor and brilliant red color. It has a slightly milder spiciness than other types of red pepper flakes, and can be located at any Asian food market or online from various retailers. If you don't have access to Korean chili flakes, then any type of crushed red pepper flakes will do.

2 pounds napa cabbage (1 average-size)

½ cup salt (I like Real Salt brand and expert fermenters recommend it, too)

12 to 14 cups water

3 scallions, thinly sliced

¼ to ⅓ cup crushed red pepper flakes (seek out Korean *gochugaru* for best flavor)

3 tablespoons grated fresh ginger

1 small Asian pear, seeded and grated

1 small peeled daikon or carrot, cut into matchsticks

4 cloves garlic, minced

Wash the napa cabbage, chop into 2-inch pieces, and place in a very large mixing bowl. Toss evenly with the salt to coat and cover with the 12 to 14 cups of water, making sure that the leaves are submerged as best as possible. Loosely cover with plastic wrap. Allow to rest for 24 hours.

Drain and rinse the cabbage thoroughly, squeezing out any excess water, and then transfer the cabbage back to the large (and cleaned) mixing bowl. Toss with the remaining ingredients (use more or less red pepper, depending on spice preference; ¼ cup makes a medium-spicy kimchi) to evenly coat and then pack tightly into a 1 gallon wide-mouth glass jar. Pack the mixture down tightly—the brine will release as the kimchi ferments.

YIELD:

16 SERVINGS

PER SERVING:

9 CALORIES

0 G FAT

219 MG SODIUM

23.6 MG POTASSIUM

2 G CARBOHYDRATES

0 G PROTEIN

Seal the jar tightly with a lid or by placing a resealable plastic bag full of water inside of the jar to weigh down and seal the kimchi. Place in a cupboard or a cool, dark place for 24 hours. Using a wooden spoon, push the cabbage under the brine to submerge the leaves every 8 to 12 hours if they wander to the top of the jar. After 24 hours, allow any gas to escape by opening the lid, and then retighten the lid and allow to rest for another 24 hours or up to 4 days. Be sure to allow the gas to escape from the jar at least once per day as the kimchi ferments. Taste the kimchi to see whether it tastes tangy enough for your liking, and once it tastes ready (like a spicy sauerkraut), transfer to the refrigerator for storage and enjoy! Kimchi will keep for up to 2 months in your refrigerator if kept in a sealed container.

This stuff can get bubbly! If you hear a fizzy sound when you open your jar of kimchi, it's a good thing; it means your fermentation is working just as it should.

Power Up Kale Salad

It's no secret that kale is considered a superfood. Full of iron and vitamins A and C, the dark leafy green also boasts a good amount of calcium and fiber. Add avocado and Parmesan Sprinkles (page 138) for some healthy fats, carrots for the vitamin A, cucumbers as a good source of copper and silica, tomatoes for their lycopene and vitamin C, and walnuts for their omega-3s, and you'll have yourself a salad that will keep you going long and strong.

5 large leaves kale, stems removed, chopped into small pieces

½ large avocado, peeled, pitted, and diced

1 tablespoon freshly squeezed lemon juice

¼ teaspoon salt

½ tablespoon Parmesan Sprinkles (page 138)

1 carrot, shredded

½ cucumber, diced

6 cherry tomatoes, sliced in half

¼ cup crushed walnuts

Place the kale in a large bowl and top evenly with avocado and lemon juice. With clean hands, massage the avocado and lemon juice into the kale until it is tender and slightly wilted. This will be very messy, but very worth it—just wash and dry your hands when you're done! Sprinkle the salad lightly with the salt and Parmesan Sprinkles, tossing gently with a fork to distribute evenly. Add the shredded carrot, cucumber, tomatoes, and walnuts and toss gently. Serve immediately.

YIELD:

4 SERVINGS

PER SERVING:

189 CALORIES

10.4 G FAT

206 MG SODIUM

1,091 MG POTASSIUM

21.1 G CARBOHYDRATES

6.3 G FIBER

7 G PROTEIN

Red Potato Watercress Salad

Watercress is such an underutilized green. It took me a long time to discover how delicious this vegetable is, as I was never exposed to it in my earlier cooking years; but once I found it, I was hooked on its tender crunch and mildly peppery and slightly sweet flavor. Rich in iron, calcium, folate, and vitamin C, this is one green that is definitely worth trying if you haven't yet done so.

3 medium-size red potatoes, peels on

2 tablespoons Stealthy Healthy Mayo (page 139)

½ tablespoon cider vinegar

1 tablespoon freshly squeezed lemon juice

½ teaspoon salt

¼ teaspoon or 3 grinds freshly ground black pepper

½ cup chopped watercress greens

3 scallions (ends removed), chopped

Scrub the potatoes and then cut into 1-inch pieces. Bring about 6 cups of water to a boil and then carefully add the potatoes. Bring the water back up to a boil and then set your timer for 9 minutes. Cook the potatoes for those 9 minutes, or until fork-tender. Drain well and then allow the potatoes to cool, at least 15 minutes.

In a small bowl, whisk together the mayo, cider vinegar, lemon juice, salt, and black pepper. Toss with the potatoes to evenly coat. Fold in the watercress and scallions and chill for 1 hour in the refrigerator before serving.

Store in an airtight container for up to 3 days.

YIELD:

4 SERVINGS

PER SERVING:

135 CALORIES

2 G FAT

361 MG SODIUM

772 MG POTASSIUM

26.8 G CARBOHYDRATES

3.4 G PROTEIN

Garlicky Rainbow Chard and Cannellinis

The colorful yellow, pink, and red stems of chard hold valuable phytonutrients called betalains. These are important as antioxidants, detoxing agents, and anti-inflammatory agents. Chard is also crazy high in vitamin K, with 1 cup providing over 600 percent of your daily recommended intake. A light sauté makes these nutritiously colorful greens even tastier. This recipe makes a fabulous light lunch or a hearty side dish.

1 bunch rainbow chard (about 7 leaves)

3 cloves garlic, minced

1 teaspoon olive oil

¾ teaspoon salt

1½ cups cooked cannellini beans, drained and rinsed

¼ teaspoon freshly ground black pepper

Wash and pat dry the chard leaves. Cut the leaves into 1½-inch pieces and the stems into slightly smaller pieces. Place in a large skillet and sprinkle with the garlic, and then drizzle with the olive oil. Sprinkle evenly with salt and sauté over medium-high heat, stirring often, until the leaves have wilted and reduced by half. Add the cannellini beans and cook for an additional 2 minutes. Top with the black pepper and serve hot.

YIELD:

4 SERVINGS

PER SERVING:

250 CALORIES

1.8 G FAT

532 MG SODIUM

981 MG POTASSIUM

43.5 G CARBOHYDRATES

17.3 G PROTEIN

Apple-Infused Shredded Brussels

Tender and slightly sweet, this recipe is a fun way to enjoy Brussels sprouts in an unconventional way. This is a wonderful dish to prepare during the fall and winter months when apple cider is plentiful.

20 Brussels sprouts

1 cup apple cider (no sugar added)

¼ teaspoon ground cinnamon

¼ teaspoon ground cardamom

¼ teaspoon freshly ground black pepper

½ teaspoon salt

To prepare the Brussels sprouts, rinse well and remove the outermost leaves. Slice the sprouts into three or four circles (they will shred apart as they cook) and arrange evenly on the bottom of a large skillet. Cover with the apple cider and then evenly top with the cinnamon, ground cardamom, black pepper, and salt. Cook over medium-high heat for 15 minutes, or until the Brussels sprouts are tender and the apple cider has reduced into a sauce, stirring halfway through the cooking time to ensure no sticking occurs and again toward the end. Serve hot.

YIELD:

4 SERVINGS

PER SERVING:

71 CALORIES

0.4 G FAT

316 MG SODIUM

447 MG POTASSIUM

16.2 G CARBOHYDRATES

3.3 G PROTEIN

Almond-Roasted Romanesco

This recipe will make your kitchen smell incredible as it's made with fragrant garlic and lemons and coated in nutritious almond meal. Romanesco is a relative of cauliflower and often can be located in the same general area in your grocer's produce section. You'll notice it right away with its vivid green fractal appearance—like a beautiful alien relative to broccoli or cauliflower. Its taste is milder than broccoli or cauliflower and slightly sweet. It also retains most of its lovely color while it cooks, which makes for an exciting presentation.

1 head romanesco (about 6 inches in diameter)

2 teaspoons olive oil

2 tablespoons almond meal

1 clove garlic, minced

¾ teaspoon salt

Juice and zest of ½ lemon

¼ teaspoon freshly ground black pepper

Preheat your oven to 400°F. Line a cookie sheet with parchment paper. Cut the romanesco into bite-size pieces, about 1 inch wide or so. Place in a bowl and toss evenly with the olive oil. Sprinkle with the almond meal evenly to cover and then spread the romanesco on the prepared cookie sheet.

Sprinkle evenly with the minced garlic, then the salt, then the lemon juice and zest, and finally the black pepper. Roast on the middle rack of the oven for about 20 minutes, or until fragrant and tender. Serve hot.

YIELD:

4 SERVINGS

PER SERVING:

55 CALORIES

3.9 G FAT

458 MG SODIUM

226 MG POTASSIUM

4.4 G CARBOHYDRATES

2 G PROTEIN

Oil-Free Roasted Broccoli

I enjoy broccoli in a variety of ways, and this is a delicious and unique way to prepare the cruciferous veggie. Broccoli is very high in vitamins C and K and adds a nice amount of fiber to your diet. Roasting the broccoli with herbes de Provence—which includes rosemary, thyme, and lavender—yields a tender yet crispy broccoli that has a subtle sweetness. This recipe makes not only a fabulous side, but also a tasty salad topper or a mix-in to pasta.

3 cups broccoli florets, separated into bite-size pieces

½ teaspoon salt

¼ teaspoon freshly ground black pepper

1 tablespoon freshly squeezed lemon juice

1 teaspoon herbes de Provence

Preheat your oven to 400°F. Place the broccoli florets in a single layer on an ungreased metal baking sheet. Sprinkle evenly with salt and black pepper and then drizzle with the lemon juice and finally with the herbes de Provence. Stir gently, then bake for 15 to 17 minutes, just until tender. Eat immediately.

YIELD:

4 SERVINGS

PER SERVING:

24 CALORIES

0.3 G FAT

314 MG SODIUM

222 MG POTASSIUM

4.7 G CARBOHYDRATES

1.9 G PROTEIN

Sweet Mustard–Glazed Rapini

Rapini (also known as broccoli rabe or raab) is a great source of vitamins A and C and high in calcium and potassium. The sweet mustard glaze in this recipe turns rapini, a typically bitter veggie, into an addictive side. I used to steer clear of rapini because of its bitterness until I realized that—much like bad attitudes—it can be tamed with a little bit of sweetness.

1 bunch rapini
(about 17 pieces)

1 tablespoon blackstrap
molasses

½ teaspoon olive oil

1 teaspoon mustard
powder

1 tablespoon pure
maple syrup

½ teaspoon salt

Rinse the rapini and cut off just the very ends of the stalks, leaving the florets, leaves, and stems attached. Pat dry, using a clean kitchen towel.

Preheat your oven to 400°F and line a large baking sheet with parchment paper (you can also leave this step out and simply use an ungreased cookie sheet). In a small bowl, whisk together the blackstrap molasses, olive oil, mustard powder, and maple syrup until well combined.

In a large bowl, toss the rapini with the molasses dressing to lightly coat and then spread on the baking sheet in a single layer. Sprinkle evenly with the salt. Bake for 17 minutes. Serve immediately.

YIELD:

6 SERVINGS

PER SERVING:

95 CALORIES

0.6 G FAT

266 MG SODIUM

59 MG POTASSIUM

16.2 G
CARBOHYDRATES

8.6 G PROTEIN

Just like the addictive appetizer found at numerous chain restaurants, this dip is delicious. Unlike that insanely unhealthy dish, this version is actually good for you! It includes nutritional yeast, an excellent source of vitamin B_{12}, which is hard to come by in a vegan diet, as well as thiamine, riboflavin, vitamin B_6, and niacin. It's free of overly processed ingredients and chock-full of delicious nutrient-dense ingredients, making it quite a healthy appetizer.

- 2 cups raw cashews, soaked in water for 2 hours and drained
- 1 cup water
- 2 tablespoons freshly squeezed lemon juice
- 1 teaspoon salt
- 2 cloves garlic, minced
- ½ cup almond meal
- ½ cup nutritional yeast flakes
- 2½ cups tightly packed chopped spinach
- 1 cup packed chopped canned (oil-free) artichoke hearts
- 3 scallions, chopped

Preheat your oven to 350°F. Place the drained cashews in a food processor along with the water, lemon juice, salt, garlic, and almond meal and blend until very smooth, about 5 minutes. Add the nutritional yeast and blend again until well combined. Transfer to a bowl and combine with the spinach, artichoke hearts, and scallions. Place in a ceramic baking dish (about 8 x 4 inches) and spread evenly. Bake for 35 minutes, or until golden brown on top. Serve warm with chips or veggies; I love this dip served with raw broccoli florets.

YIELD:

10 SERVINGS

PER SERVING:

225 CALORIES

15.6 G FAT

265 MG SODIUM

502 MG POTASSIUM

16.2 G CARBOHYDRATES

9.8 G PROTEIN

Cheesy BBQ Kale Chips

Kale chips are crispy, crunchy, and far lower in calories than potato chips. This recipe is a breeze to make and much cheaper than store bought-kale chips. No need for a dehydrator to make these addictive morsels; simply use a low temperature on your oven and keep a close eye on them as they cook.

15 medium-size curly kale leaves, stemmed

3 tablespoons Beyond Good BBQ Sauce (page 101)

2 teaspoons freshly squeezed lime juice

1 teaspoon ground chili seasoning

1 teaspoon salt

⅓ cup nutritional yeast flakes

⅛ teaspoon freshly ground black pepper

Preheat your oven to 200°F and cover two large baking sheets with parchment paper. Rinse and dry the kale leaves very well, patting each leaf down with a kitchen towel to get it totally dry; starting with very dry kale leaves is key to crispy kale chips. Even the slightest bit of water can lead to soggy results.

Rip the kale into equal-size pieces (about 2 x 2 inches; I find that bigger pieces work better than smaller) and toss gently with the barbecue sauce and lime juice until completely coated.

In a small bowl, combine the chili seasoning, salt, nutritional yeast flakes, and black pepper. Dust the kale with the mixture until coated on both sides. Arrange in a single layer on the baking sheet so that no kale leaves are overlapping.

Bake on the middle rack for 30 minutes, flip, and bake for an additional 30 to 60 minutes, until crispy and completely dried. Let cool before enjoying.

YIELD:

8 SERVINGS

PER SERVING:

48 CALORIES

0.4 G FAT

371 MG SODIUM

309 MG POTASSIUM

8.8 G CARBOHYDRATES

3.9 G PROTEIN

Strawberry Banana Green Smoothie

This simple smoothie is packed full of greens, but the only thing you'll taste is sweet strawberry banana goodness. I recommend using a mild-tasting and tender green, such as spinach. Strawberries are high in both antioxidants and anti-inflammatory nutrients. Studies show that two days or less of fresh strawberry storage time is best to maximize the nutritional benefits of the fruit. This is a great reason to visit a strawberry patch or seek out farmers' markets when strawberries are in season and freeze a few bags of berries for later use throughout the year.

2 bananas, peeled and frozen

4 fresh strawberries, greens on, or ⅔ cup frozen

1½ cups packed spinach or baby kale

2 Medjool dates, pitted

1½ cups cold nondairy milk (recommended: almond), plus more to thin if necessary

Place all the ingredients in a blender and blend until very smooth. Pour into two 16-ounce glasses and enjoy immediately.

YIELD:

2 SERVINGS

PER SERVING:

84 CALORIES

0.4 G FAT

8 MG SODIUM

301 MG POTASSIUM

20.1 G CARBOHYDRATES

1.2 G PROTEIN

Mint Chocolate Chip Smoothie

If you're looking for an indulgent dessert that's also healthy, look no further! This smoothie is brimming with mint chocolaty flavor and a nice dose of greens from the addition of fresh spinach and mint leaves. For those who may be side-eyeing the spinach, trust me, you won't even be able to tell it's in there!

½ cup packed spinach

2 tablespoons packed fresh mint

1 average-size banana, frozen

2 Medjool dates, pitted

1 tablespoon unsweetened cocoa powder

1¼ cups unsweetened almond milk

½ tablespoon cacao nibs

Place the spinach, mint, banana, dates, cocoa powder, and almond milk in a blender and blend until very smooth, stopping and scraping down the sides of the blender container as needed. Once smooth, add the cacao nibs and pulse a few times until blended. Serve immediately.

YIELD:

2 SERVINGS

PER SERVING:

184 CALORIES

4.5 G FAT

62 MG SODIUM

534 MG POTASSIUM

32.1 G CARBOHYDRATES

8.4 G PROTEIN

Walnut Arugula Pesto

Pesto is a favorite accompaniment of mine, although I never make it using a traditional recipe, which includes pine nuts and Parmigiano-Reggiano. Instead I like to add different greens to supplement the basil—this recipe has arugula—and I prefer the flavor of a heartier nut, such as walnuts. This version works beautifully and still includes enough basil to call it pesto.

½ cup walnuts

2 cloves garlic, roasted (see sidebar)

2 cups packed arugula

2 cups packed fresh basil leaves

3 tablespoons olive oil

¼ teaspoon salt

¼ cup water

¼ cup Parmesan Sprinkles (page 138)

Preheat your oven to 375°F and place the walnuts on a rimmed cookie sheet. Bake for 7 minutes, or until fragrant. Place the roasted garlic, toasted walnuts, arugula, basil, olive oil, salt, water, and Parmesan sprinkles in a food processor and blend until very smooth, 1 to 2 minutes, stopping and scraping down the sides of the bowl as needed. Use on pasta, as a sandwich accompaniment, or as an added burst of flavor to soups and stews.

YIELD:

8 SERVINGS

PER SERVING:

113 CALORIES

10.6 G FAT

77 MG SODIUM

154 MG POTASSIUM

3 G CARBOHYDRATES

3.6 G PROTEIN

To easily roast garlic, place the cloves in a foil pouch and bake at 400°F for 30 minutes, or until tender and fragrant. You can roast an entire bulb this way by simply cutting the bottom off the cloves to expose just a bit of the garlic cloves within. Refrigerate for up to 2 weeks and use as needed.

Greenest Goddess Dressing

Modeled after the bottled versions of green goddess dressing, which usually have buttermilk, egg, and lots of oil, this version is much healthier and tastier with fresh ingredients and extra greens for good measure. One of the main ingredients in this dressing is tarragon, which has a slightly sweet, licorice-like flavor. You can find tarragon along with other fresh herbs at most supermarkets.

1 avocado, peeled and pitted

2 scallions, chopped

¼ cup fresh tarragon leaves

2 tablespoons cider vinegar

¼ cup fresh parsley leaves

2 tablespoons chopped fresh chives

1 small clove garlic, peeled

¾ cup water

½ teaspoon salt

Place all the ingredients in a blender and blend until very smooth. Store in an airtight container for up to 1 week.

YIELD:

10 SERVINGS

PER SERVING:

46 CALORIES

4 G FAT

127 MG SODIUM

140 MG POTASSIUM

2.5 G CARBOHYDRATES

0.7 G PROTEIN

CHAPTER 2

HEARTY GRAINS

Ceres is the Greek goddess of harvest and agriculture, and her name is where we get the word *cereal*, which is synonymous with the word *grain* in its most general usage. Grains have been a part of the human diet for thousands of years, and there is a plethora of grains beyond wheat. Grains are basically any type of food stuff, such as the seed and/or husk of the seed of certain plants, which can be easily dried and stored for human consumption.

Cereal grains include sorghum, corn, millet, oats, rice, teff, and wild rice. Amaranth, quinoa, and buckwheat are classified as pseudograins. All these grains are gluten free. With minimal processing—eaten as a whole grain—grains are high in vitamins, minerals, fats, and protein in addition to being filling and high in insoluble fiber. In this chapter, you'll find recipes that feature more commonly known grains, such as brown rice (Not-So-Dirty Rice, page 51) and oats (Get Up and Go Granola, page 58), as well as grains that may be less familiar, such as teff (Chocolate Brownie Cake, page 69) and sorghum (Cinnamon Pumpkin Donuts, page 63).

Three-Grain Breakfast Medley

This easy recipe made with kasha, quinoa, and millet is perfect for breakfast, a light lunch, or a simple sweet snack. It's a great way to cook kasha (toasted buckwheat groats) as the firmer grains, quinoa and millet, help keep it from getting mushy, a common complaint with kasha sold in the United States, which varies slightly from kasha that is available outside of the country.

¼ cup kasha

¼ cup uncooked red or white quinoa, rinsed

¼ cup uncooked millet, rinsed

1 cup water

½ cup unsweetened almond milk

¼ teaspoon salt

¼ cup dried blueberries or raisins

2 tablespoons pure maple syrup, or to taste

½ teaspoon pure vanilla extract

½ teaspoon ground cinnamon

In a small saucepan, combine the kasha, quinoa, millet, water, almond milk, and salt and mix well to combine. Stir in the dried blueberries. Over medium-high heat, bring to a boil. Once at a boil, stir and then cover with a lid, lower the heat to low, and simmer for 15 minutes, stirring occasionally. Remove from the heat, keeping the lid on the pot, and allow to rest for 5 minutes. Fluff gently with a fork. Stir in the maple syrup, vanilla extract, and cinnamon. Serve immediately or allow to cool to room temperature before serving.

YIELD:

4 SERVINGS

PER SERVING:

158 CALORIES

2 G FAT

162 MG SODIUM

92 MG POTASSIUM

29.6 G CARBOHYDRATES

4.9 G PROTEIN

Goji Overnight Oats

Overnight oats have gained quite a bit of popularity in the healthy eating sphere, and they are a fun twist on traditional preparations of oatmeal. To make true overnight oats, pick steel-cut oats (which can stand up to soaking for 8 hours without getting mushy). If using rolled oats, I suggest soaking them for only an hour or so, so they retain much of the oats' texture. Considered a fruit as well as an herb, goji berries are fat free, high in fiber, and full of antioxidants, and they are an easy natural sweetener for oatmeal and so much more. If you don't have gojis handy, raisins, dried blueberries, or dried cherries also taste great.

¼ cup dried goji berries

¼ cup finely chopped pecans

½ teaspoon ground cinnamon

2 teaspoons golden flaxseeds

1 cup certified gluten-free oats (rolled or steel-cut)

1½ cups unsweetened almond milk

1 to 2 tablespoons pure maple syrup

Place all the ingredients, except the maple syrup, in a medium-size bowl and stir well. Cover tightly with plastic wrap and place in the refrigerator for 1 to 2 hours if using rolled oats and about 8 hours if using steel-cut oats (the liquid will still remain if using steel-cut), until tender. Sweeten with 1 to 2 tablespoons of maple syrup.

YIELD:

4 SERVINGS

PER SERVING:

239 CALORIES

4.5 G FAT

32 MG SODIUM

175 MG POTASSIUM

32.3 G CARBOHYDRATES

7.6 G PROTEIN

Choco-Chip, PB, & Banana Oatmeal (a.k.a. My Favorite Oatmeal) OF

There's a reason I call this recipe "My Favorite Oatmeal." Not only is it as filling as it is tasty, I get to indulge each morning in a bowl full of goodness that tastes much more like dessert than like plain ol' oatmeal. With banana as the sweetener and chocolaty cacao nibs dotted throughout, this breakfast dish gets me excited and ready for the day like no other meal. Bonus—it takes under five minutes to make!

⅓ cup certified gluten-free rolled oats (I like Bob's Red Mill Extra Thick Rolled Oats)

½ cup water

½ teaspoon pure vanilla extract

2 teaspoons date sugar

2 teaspoons peanut or almond butter

1 banana, sliced

½ teaspoon cacao nibs

In a very small saucepan, combine the oats, water, vanilla extract, and date sugar. Cook over medium-high heat until thickened, about 2 minutes. Stir often as it cooks so the oats don't stick to the pan. Once cooked, stir in the peanut butter and transfer to a cereal bowl. Top with the banana, and fold to combine. Sprinkle with the cacao nibs and devour.

YIELD:

1 SERVING

PER SERVING:

298 CALORIES

FAT:

8.3 G

54 MG SODIUM

506 MG POTASSIUM

53.7 G CARBOHYDRATES

7.4 G PROTEIN

Not-So-Dirty Rice

This semispicy dish is a great way to jazz up brown rice. It's a cleaned-up version of the classic dish "dirty rice," which traditionally features such ingredients as giblets or liver. The jalapeño called for adds a touch of heat, but not too much—the heat of individual peppers can vary, so taste your jalapeño before you add it to see how spicy it is. Feel free to adjust to your preference for piquant, and just leave out the jalapeño if you prefer the flavor mild.

1 teaspoon olive oil

1 large shallot or small red onion, diced

½ jalapeño pepper, seeded and diced (omit for zero heat)

2 stalks celery, diced

1 carrot, diced

2 cloves garlic, minced

Salt

2 teaspoons ground chili seasoning

1 teaspoon dried oregano

½ teaspoon lemon zest

½ cup water

3 cups cooked brown rice

¼ cup packed chopped fresh parsley

¼ cup Parmesan Sprinkles (page 138)

In a medium-size skillet, heat the oil over medium-high heat and add the shallot, jalapeño, celery, carrot, and garlic. Sprinkle with 1 teaspoon of the salt and sauté for about 3 minutes, stirring often. Add the chili seasoning, oregano, lemon zest, and water and lower the heat to medium. Allow the mixture to simmer until the vegetables are cooked and the mixture has thickened, about 5 minutes. Stir into the cooked rice and then fold in the parsley. Add salt to taste, if desired. Top with Parmesan Sprinkles and serve hot.

YIELD:

8 SERVINGS

PER SERVING:

292 CALORIES

3.8 G FAT

323 MG SODIUM

300 MG POTASSIUM

57.9 G CARBOHYDRATES

6.8 G PROTEIN

Wild Rice Pilaf

Wild rice is a species of grass that is related distantly to Asian varieties of rice. It is high in protein and fiber and has a distinctively chewy outside with a tender inside. This wild rice dish has a toothsome texture and mild nutty flavor that melds perfectly with the slight sweetness of blueberries and blackstrap molasses. Let the dish rest for a couple of hours for best flavor.

3 tablespoons white balsamic vinegar

3 tablespoons freshly squeezed orange juice

1 tablespoon blackstrap molasses

½ teaspoon salt

2 cups cooked wild rice

¾ cup chopped walnuts

¾ cup blueberries

½ cup chopped fresh parsley

In a small bowl, whisk together the balsamic vinegar, orange juice, blackstrap molasses, and salt. In a medium-size bowl, toss together the wild rice, walnuts, blueberries, and parsley until evenly combined. Drizzle with the dressing and toss well to evenly coat. Chill for at least 2 hours in the refrigerator and then toss again before serving.

YIELD:

7 SERVINGS

PER SERVING:

269 CALORIES

8.5 G FAT

174 MG SODIUM

361 MG POTASSIUM

41 G CARBOHYDRATES

10.2 G PROTEIN

Red Quinoa Tabbouleh

Tabbouleh is traditionally made with bulgur, a variety of wheat, but this gluten-free recipe features quinoa in place of bulgur. Parsley is the star of the show in tabbouleh, so seek out fresh, crisp, green leaves for an extra tasty result. You can certainly use white quinoa in this recipe if you'd like, but I love the vibrant color that red quinoa adds to this already colorful dish.

1 cup uncooked red quinoa, rinsed

2 cups water

1 clove garlic, crushed

1 teaspoon salt

2 tablespoons freshly squeezed lemon juice

2 tablespoons olive oil

½ teaspoon paprika

1 cup packed chopped fresh parsley

2 tomatoes, diced

1 cup diced cucumber

¼ cup chopped fresh mint

2 tablespoons chopped fresh chives

In a medium-size saucepan, bring the quinoa, water, and crushed garlic to a boil. Cover, lower the heat, and simmer for 15 minutes, or until all the water is absorbed. Remove from the heat and discard the garlic.

Allow the quinoa to cool for about 15 minutes, and then add the salt, lemon juice, olive oil, and paprika. Transfer to a large bowl and toss with the rest of the ingredients. Enjoy immediately or chill for 1 to 2 hours before serving.

YIELD:

6 SERVINGS

PER SERVING:

162 CALORIES

6.7 G FAT

402 MG SODIUM

371 MG POTASSIUM

21.8 G CARBOHYDRATES

5 G PROTEIN

Summertime Quinoa Bowl

This medley doesn't need many ingredients to give it a whole lot of flavor. Although dried oregano can be used (use about 1 teaspoon), fresh leaves truly take this dish over the top. This is best enjoyed during the summer months when both zucchini and tomatoes are in season.

1 cup uncooked quinoa, rinsed

2 cups salted vegan vegetable broth, such as Super Easy Veggie Broth (page 171)

1 zucchini, sliced into ½-inch-wide coins and then halved

1 cup cherry or grape tomatoes

¼ cup diced red onion

1 tablespoon chopped fresh oregano

2 teaspoons olive oil

½ teaspoon salt

In a medium-size pot, bring the quinoa and vegetable broth to a boil, stirring often. Lower the heat to medium-low and simmer for 15 minutes, or until all the liquid has absorbed.

While the quinoa simmers, in a medium-size skillet, toss together the zucchini, cherry tomatoes, diced onion, oregano, and olive oil. Sprinkle with the salt and sauté over medium-high heat until all the vegetables are tender, about 7 minutes. Add the cooked quinoa to the pan and toss gently to combine.

Serve hot.

YIELD:

4 SERVINGS

PER SERVING:

218 CALORIES

5.9 G FAT

682 MG SODIUM

607 MG POTASSIUM

32.5 G CARBOHYDRATES

9.6 G PROTEIN

Most granola is made with some oil to get the crispy crunchy texture. This recipe is great for those who are avoiding oil, as it uses chia to bind and crisp the oats to toasty granola perfection.

2 cups certified gluten-free rolled oats

⅔ cup raisins or other dried fruit

¼ cup sunflower seeds

2 tablespoons ground chia seeds

3 tablespoons water

⅓ cup agave or pure maple syrup

½ teaspoon salt

¼ cup goji berries or dried cherries

Preheat your oven to 325°F. Line a large baking sheet with parchment paper or a silicone mat. Place the oats in a large mixing bowl along with the raisins and sunflower seeds.

In a medium-size bowl, stir together the ground chia seeds with the water and allow to rest for 2 minutes, until gelled. Add the agave and salt to the chia gel. Pour the chia gel over the oat mixture and toss to coat. Spread in an even layer on the prepared baking sheet and bake for 25 minutes. Use a spatula to flip the granola over and bake for an additional 10 minutes, or until golden and crunchy. Toss with the goji berries. Let cool completely before enjoying.

YIELD:

8 SERVINGS

PER SERVING:

173 CALORIES

3 G FAT

149 MG SODIUM

100 MG POTASSIUM

35.4 G CARBOHYDRATES

3.6 G PROTEIN

Blackberry Coconut Quinoa

This easy treat is delicious all by its lonesome, and it also makes a fabulous addition to yogurt, cereal, and ice cream. Its texture is what draws me in most, with the coconut taking on a slightly chewy texture once ground, mixed with the blackberries, and allowed to chill. Blackberries are high in vitamins C and K as well as fiber. This recipe makes a fast and filling snack between meals and keeps for up to 4 days in the refrigerator.

⅓ cup dried unsweetened coconut chips/flakes

¼ cup cooked quinoa

¼ teaspoon pure vanilla extract

1 cup blackberries

¼ cup pomegranate arils

⅓ cup blueberries

Place the coconut chips in a clean spice grinder and grind just until crumbly. In a medium-size bowl, toss the quinoa with the vanilla extract, stir in the blackberries, pomegranate arils, and blueberries, and gently fold in the ground coconut chips.

Chill for 1 hour and then serve cold.

YIELD:

8 SERVINGS

PER SERVING:

99 CALORIES

5.9 G FAT

4 MG SODIUM

123 MG POTASSIUM

11 G CARBOHYDRATES

1.6 G PROTEIN

Cherry Almond Millet

This recipe is a lot like rice pudding—sweet, tender, and utterly addictive—but made with millet instead, which gives the dish a heartier texture and bolder, almost nutty, flavor. Cherries, a good source of fiber and vitamin C, stud the dish adding a touch of tart and sweet.

2 cups water

1 cup uncooked millet, soaked in water for 1 hour and drained

⅓ cup date or coconut palm sugar

Pinch of ground cinnamon

1 teaspoon pure vanilla extract

1 tablespoon pure maple syrup

¼ cup unsweetened almond milk

¼ cup almond meal

15 to 20 sweet cherries, pitted and coarsely chopped

In a 2-quart saucepan, bring the water to a boil. Immediately stir in the drained millet and date sugar and lower the heat to low. Cover and simmer until the millet is tender, about 20 minutes.

Stir in the cinnamon, vanilla extract, maple syrup, almond milk, almond meal, and cherries. Cook over medium heat just until thickened, stirring often to avoid sticking, and then allow to cool completely before serving.

Store in an airtight container for up to 3 days in the refrigerator.

YIELD:

6 SERVINGS

PER SERVING:

229 CALORIES

3.6 G FAT

18 MG SODIUM

146 MG POTASSIUM

44.9 G CARBOHYDRATES

4.7 G PROTEIN

Chocolate Teff Waffles

These little waffles pack a nutritional punch with the addition of high-protein teff flour, which is made from the tiniest grain in the world. It has a slightly sweet and almost chocolaty flavor that works really well in chocolate-flavored gluten-free recipes. Cook these slightly longer than you would regular waffles to ensure they are totally cooked throughout.

2 tablespoons flaxseed meal

2 cups plus 2 tablespoons water

½ teaspoon olive or coconut oil or nonstick cooking spray

⅓ cup unsweetened Dutch-processed cocoa powder

1½ cups teff flour

2½ teaspoons baking powder

¾ teaspoons salt

4 tablespoons coconut or olive oil

¼ cup pure maple syrup or coconut palm sugar

In a small bowl, mix together the flaxseed meal and the 2 tablespoons of water and let rest until gelled, about 5 minutes. Preheat a standard-size waffle iron. Lightly grease if not using nonstick.

In a large mixing bowl, whisk together the cocoa powder, teff flour, baking powder, and salt. Stir in the coconut oil, maple syrup, and remaining 2 cups of water. Using a whisk, mix well until completely smooth. Drop ¼ cup of the batter into the waffle iron and cook for about 4 minutes per waffle. Increase the time by about 1 minute if using a Belgian waffle maker. Let cool briefly before serving; these are best enjoyed hot. Makes about six standard-size waffles.

YIELD:

6 SERVINGS

PER SERVING:

137 CALORIES

9 G FAT

298 MG SODIUM

377 MG POTASSIUM

13.1 G CARBOHYDRATES

3.3 G PROTEIN

Cinnamon Pumpkin Donuts

Finally, a donut you can feel good about eating! A true treat for breakfast or dessert, these delicious pumpkin donuts are soft and lightly spiced with cinnamon and each donut boasts a good amount of protein from both the chickpea and buckwheat flours. You'll need a donut pan for this recipe, which you can usually pick up at any department store or well-stocked food market for around $6.

¼ teaspoon olive or coconut oil, for pan

1 tablespoon ground chia seeds

¾ cup plus 2 tablespoons water

½ cup chickpea flour

½ cup sorghum flour

¼ cup buckwheat flour

1 teaspoon baking powder

½ teaspoon baking soda

¾ teaspoon salt

1 teaspoon ground cinnamon

¼ cup coconut palm sugar

½ cup canned pure pumpkin puree

¼ cup pure maple syrup

1 teaspoon pure vanilla extract

1 teaspoon ground cinnamon

2 tablespoons olive or coconut oil

Preheat your oven to 375°F. Lightly oil a six- to eight-count donut pan (or use a nonstick donut pan). In a small bowl, combine the ground chia seeds with the 2 tablespoons of water and allow to rest for about 5 minutes, until gelled.

In a large bowl, whisk together the chickpea flour, sorghum flour, buckwheat flour, baking powder, baking soda, salt, cinnamon, and palm sugar. Make a well in the center of the dry ingredients and add the pumpkin puree, maple syrup, vanilla extract, cinnamon, remaining ¾ cup of water, and olive oil. Whisk vigorously until smooth and then mix in the gelled chia seeds until very well combined. Distribute the batter evenly among the donut pan indentions, making sure not to overfill the cups. Bake for 17 to 20 minutes, or until spongy and fragrant. Let cool for at least 15 minutes and then loosen gently by running a knife around the edges before inverting and enjoying.

YIELD:

6 SERVINGS

PER SERVING:

226 CALORIES

6.4 G FAT

421 MG SODIUM

290 MG POTASSIUM

40 G CARBOHYDRATES

5.2 G PROTEIN

If you don't have a donut pan handy, make these into muffins by using a standard-size muffin pan, doubling the recipe to make twelve muffins and baking at 350°F for 25 to 30 minutes.

Cinnamon Bun Milk Shake

This frosty milk shake is a true treat. Even though this shake isn't made with ice cream, it sure tastes as if it is! Instead, it's made with frozen bananas, flaxseeds, and oats, and is quite filling, making it a perfect choice for an easy breakfast or a healthy dessert.

2 bananas, peeled and frozen

1 teaspoon flaxseeds

2 Medjool dates, pitted

½ cup certified gluten-free rolled oats

1½ teaspoons ground cinnamon

1 teaspoon pure vanilla extract

2 cups cold unsweetened almond milk

Place all the ingredients in a blender and blend until very smooth, stopping and scraping down the sides of the blender container as needed. Serve immediately.

YIELD:

4 SERVINGS

PER SERVING:

151 CALORIES

3.5 G FAT

43 MG SODIUM

371 MG POTASSIUM

24.5 G CARBOHYDRATES

7 G PROTEIN

Banana Oatmeal Raisin Cookies

I love these cookies for their simple ingredients, their easy prep (my six-year-old loves making these with me and can make the cookie dough all on her own), and their irresistible flavor. Pack a few of these away in your bag for road trips, office snacks, or a quick treat when you're on the go. Bananas are very high in soluble fiber, which is directly connected to lower risk of heart disease and provides digestive benefits by keeping everything moving along nicely. One study claims that eating just two bananas per day can increase your body's bifidobacteria, which helps regulate gastrointestinal systems.

2 small bananas

1 teaspoon pure vanilla extract

¼ teaspoon salt

½ teaspoon ground cinnamon

1¼ cups certified gluten-free rolled oats

⅓ cup golden raisins

Preheat the oven to 350°F and line a baking sheet with parchment paper. In a large bowl, mash the bananas until smooth, using a potato masher or large fork. Stir in the vanilla extract, salt, and cinnamon. Fold in the oats until well combined. The mixture shouldn't be runny, so if your bananas are larger, you may need to add more oats. Fold in the raisins and allow the batter to rest for 7 minutes. Drop the batter by the tablespoonful about 2 inches apart onto the prepared baking sheet and then shape gently into cookies. Bake for 15 minutes, or until edges are lightly browned. Let cool briefly before enjoying.

YIELD:

16 SERVINGS

PER SERVING:

51 CALORIES

0.6 G FAT

35 MG SODIUM

76 MG POTASSIUM

10.9 G CARBOHYDRATES

1.3 G PROTEIN

Chocolate Brownie Cake

This chocolate cake is quite a delight, and it happens to be oil free, low in calories, and low in fat. It will make you think of dessert in a brand-new light. Just serve this delightful cake to guests (or unsuspecting family members) and see whether they can tell it's closer to health food than junk food. My littlest says it tastes just like a brownie, and I don't disagree. Slather on some Oh-So-Rich Chocolate Glaze (page 70) for an extra-indulgent treat.

1 banana, mashed (about ⅔ cup)

1 teaspoon pure vanilla extract

½ cup unsweetened applesauce

⅓ cup unrefined sugar, such as maple or coconut palm

⅓ cup agave syrup

½ cup unsweetened natural or Dutch-processed cocoa powder

1 teaspoon baking soda

1 teaspoon baking powder

½ teaspoon salt

⅔ cup teff flour

1 cup chickpea flour

1 cup water

Preheat your oven to 350°F and line the bottom and the sides of an 8-inch square cake pan with parchment paper. To easily do this, cut two strips 8 inches wide x 12 inches long and crisscross them over each other to completely cover the pan.

In a large mixing bowl, whisk together the mashed banana, vanilla extract, applesauce, unrefined sugar, agave, cocoa powder, baking soda, baking powder, and salt. Gradually add the teff flour and chickpea flour along with the water and mix well until a smooth batter is formed. Pour the batter into the prepared cake pan and bake for 30 minutes, or until firm to the touch. Let cool briefly and then serve. Enjoy plain or top with chocolate glaze and/or fresh fruit.

YIELD:

16 SERVINGS

PER SERVING:

112 CALORIES

1.3 G FAT

167 MG SODIUM

241 MG POTASSIUM

24.2 G CARBOHYDRATES

3.7 G PROTEIN

WITH CHOCOLATE GLAZE:

126 CALORIES

1.5 G FAT

202 MG SODIUM

283 MG POTASSIUM

27.5 G CARBOHYDRATES

3.9 G PROTEIN

Oh-So-Rich Chocolate Glaze

If you're a fan of dark chocolate, you'll love this sultry glaze. Use this easy recipe as a topping for cakes (it's a perfect match for the Chocolate Brownie Cake, page 69) or as a decadent dip for fresh fruits, such as strawberries.

¼ cup unsweetened cocoa powder

1 teaspoon pure vanilla extract

¼ teaspoon salt

3 tablespoons pure maple syrup

Place all the ingredients in a small bowl and whisk together until smooth. Store in an airtight container for up to 2 weeks.

YIELD:

16 SERVINGS

PER SERVING:

14 CALORIES

0.2 G FAT

35 MG SODIUM

42 MG POTASSIUM

3.3 CARBOHYDRATES

0.2 G PROTEIN

CHAPTER 3

FABULOUS FRUITS

These recipes highlight the vast assortment of naturally sweet fruits, such as apples, bananas, berries, and coconuts, and not-so-sweet fruits, such as plantains and tomatoes. The word *fruit* also encapsulates a few foods beyond what we normally consider fruits—such as eggplants, peppers, and avocados. These foods are mostly low in fat and high in fiber and many of them will help curb your sweet tooth when a craving strikes. They're also incredibly versatile and even sweeter fruits can be used in so many dishes beyond just desserts—check out the Kabocha, Apple, and Fennel Bisque (page 79) or Roasted Grape and Asparagus Salad (page 75). Fruits also make fabulous snacks all by themselves, and we keep a giant fruit bowl filled at all times in my house. It's a colorful and cheerful reminder to get enough fruits throughout the day!

Light and Lemony Fusilli with Asparagus and Roasted Tomatoes

The bright flavor of lemon in this pasta makes this a lovely light dish for dinner or lunch. This pasta is brilliantly easy and oil free, thanks to the easy hummus recipe on page 157. In a pinch, you may use store-bought hummus, which adds a small amount of oil but an extra dose of convenience.

16 to 20 stalks asparagus

2 cups cherry tomatoes

1 teaspoon vegan vegetable bouillon powder

1 teaspoon salt

2 cloves garlic, minced, or 1 teaspoon garlic powder

¼ teaspoon freshly ground black pepper

1 tablespoon plus 2 teaspoons freshly squeezed lemon juice

1 (12-ounce) package brown rice fusilli pasta

⅔ cups Oil-Free Hummus (page 157), or store-bought

⅓ cup finely chopped fresh parsley

Preheat your oven to 425°F. Line a large baking sheet with parchment paper or a silicone mat. Trim the tough ends from the asparagus and then cut the stalks evenly into pieces about 2 inches long.

In a large bowl, toss the asparagus and cherry tomatoes with the vegetable bouillon powder, ½ teaspoon salt, and minced garlic to evenly coat. Sprinkle evenly with the black pepper and then drizzle with the 2 teaspoons of lemon juice. Arrange in an even layer on the prepared baking sheet. Bake for 20 to 25 minutes, until the vegetables are tender.

Meanwhile, cook the pasta according to the package directions and then rinse well with cold water. Place back in the pot and douse with the 1 tablespoon of lemon juice, the remaining ½ teaspoon salt, and the hummus, taking care to evenly coat but to not break the pasta by overstirring. Gently fold in the parsley and then the vegetable mixture.

YIELD:

8 SERVINGS

PER SERVING:

205 CALORIES

3.3 G FAT

401 MG SODIUM

259 MG POTASSIUM

39.5 G CARBOHYDRATES

6.3 G PROTEIN

Roasted Grape and Asparagus Salad

Roasting is an exciting way to enjoy the oh-so-common grape; the long oven time brings out even more of a grape's sweetness. Grapes are high in vitamin K, which is essential to healthy blood and promotes stronger bones. They are also a good source of vitamin C. Paired with asparagus and served on a bed of collard ribbons, this salad is as healthful and filling as it is unusual.

20 stalks asparagus

1 cup seedless red grapes

¾ teaspoon olive oil

½ teaspoon poppy seeds

¼ teaspoon freshly ground black pepper

3 collard green leaves

1 tablespoon freshly squeezed lemon juice

½ teaspoon salt

2 teaspoons pure maple syrup

¼ cup pine nuts

Preheat your oven to 400°F and line a large baking sheet with parchment paper or a silicone mat. Trim the tough ends from the asparagus and cut the stalks into thirds. Place on the prepared baking sheet along with the grapes. Drizzle evenly with the olive oil and sprinkle with the poppy seeds and black pepper. Bake for 17 to 20 minutes, until the asparagus is tender.

Remove the stems from the collard leaves and then stack the leaves on top of each other and roll into a cylinder. Slice thinly to chiffonade the greens into ribbons. Massage the greens with the lemon juice, salt, and maple syrup for about 1 minute, until tender. Toss with the roasted grapes and asparagus and add the pine nuts. Serve immediately.

YIELD:

6 SERVINGS

PER SERVING:

86 CALORIES

4.8 G FAT

198 MG SODIUM

202 MG POTASSIUM

10 G CARBOHYDRATES

2.7 G PROTEIN

Dilly Avocado Toasts OF

When friends come to visit, I like to break out the fancy, and these toasts fit the bill nicely with their brilliant colors and crisp lemony dill flavor. Serve these beauties alongside a hot cup of coffee in the morning or a nice mug of tea in the afternoon for a stunning (and easy) breakfast or snack. Avocados are high in vitamin B_6 and fiber. Test for ripeness by gently pressing the skin of the fruit. If it gives easily to gentle pressure under your thumb, it is ripe. If not, let it ripen for a day or two at room temperature. Keep ripe avocados fresher longer by storing in the refrigerator once they have ripened.

4 slices whole-grain gluten-free bread

1 avocado, peeled and pitted

¼ teaspoon salt

¼ teaspoon white balsamic vinegar

½ teaspoon lemon zest

2 radishes, thinly sliced

2 tablespoons chopped fresh dill

1 tablespoon sunflower seeds

Preheat your oven to BROIL and place the slices of bread on a metal baking sheet. Broil for 3 to 5 minutes, until the bread is golden brown, flipping after 2 minutes. (Alternatively, you can use a toaster for this step!)

In a small bowl, mash the flesh of the avocado with the salt, balsamic vinegar, and lemon zest. Spread the avocado evenly on the toast and artfully arrange the radishes, dill, and sunflower seeds. Enjoy immediately.

YIELD:

4 SERVINGS

PER SERVING:

181 CALORIES

12.2 G FAT

284 MG SODIUM

306 MG POTASSIUM

16.5 G CARBOHYDRATES

3.4 G PROTEIN

Kabocha, Apple, and Fennel Bisque

Kabocha squash (also known as Japanese pumpkin), with its striking green skin and bright orange flesh, is similar to butternut squash in flavor, but is a touch sweeter. This smooth bisque has a lightly sweet flavor from both the apple and kabocha, and the fresh garlic adds a zesty bite, so if you prefer a milder flavor, reduce to one garlic clove or use roasted garlic in place of fresh raw garlic. This nourishing soup is high in vitamins A, B_6, and C. For an extra explosion of flavor, add a teaspoon or so of fennel greens and red apple peel slivers to garnish before serving.

1 medium-size kabocha squash (yields 3 to 4 cups)

1 apple, cored and chopped (reserve 1 square inch of peel for garnish)

2 cloves garlic

3 cups low-sodium vegan vegetable broth, plus more, if needed, or Super Easy Veggie Broth (page 171), salt omitted

¼ cup chopped fennel bulb (chop the white part; save the greens for garnish)

1 teaspoon salt, or to taste

Preheat your oven to 400°F.

Using a fork, evenly poke about twenty holes in the kabocha squash. Roast the squash by placing on a cookie sheet on the middle rack of your oven. Bake for 30 to 40 minutes, or until fork-tender. Slice the cooked squash in half and discard the seeds. Scoop out the flesh, using a spoon, and place in a blender. Add the chopped apple, garlic cloves, vegetable broth, and chopped fennel. Puree until very smooth, adding more vegetable broth, if needed, to thin.

Add the salt and blend again to evenly distribute.

Warm over medium heat, or serve as is, garnished with the reserved fennel greens and apple peel.

YIELD:

6 SERVINGS

PER SERVING:

64 CALORIES

0.7 G FAT

585 MG SODIUM

148 MG POTASSIUM

14.1 G CARBOHYDRATES

0.8 G PROTEIN

Creaty Tomato Bisque

Tomatoes are rich in lycopene, an antioxidant that gives the fruits their color. According to the American Cancer Society, people who often enjoy foods rich in lycopene have lower incidents of cancer and heart disease. Use your blender over a food processor, if you have one, for this recipe as it makes for an insanely creamy soup. With this bisque, the creamier, the better.

1 (28-ounce) can crushed tomatoes

1 cup raw cashews, soaked in water for 2 hours and drained

1 small clove garlic

½ plus ⅛ teaspoon salt

1 teaspoon fresh tarragon

1 cup water

Place all the ingredients in a blender and blend until very smooth, making sure to stop and scrape down the sides of the blender container as needed. Transfer to a 2- to 3-quart saucepan and heat gently over medium heat until the bisque reaches your desired temperature.

Store in an airtight container in the refrigerator for up to 1 week or freeze for up to 3 months.

YIELD:

5 SERVINGS

PER SERVING:

223 CALORIES

12.7 G FAT

615 MG SODIUM

159 MG POTASSIUM

21.7 G CARBOHYDRATES

8 G PROTEIN

Plantain Tacos

Make these tacos for breakfast, lunch, or dinner for a special dish that features the banana doppelgänger. The plantain will be ready to cook when the skin is yellow with brown spots, indicating a firm but slightly soft and sweet fruit that works wonderfully in savory dishes.

1 large plantain, peeled

½ teaspoon olive oil

Salt

1½ tablespoons water

1 cup cooked red beans, drained and rinsed

1 teaspoon garlic powder

½ teaspoon ground cumin

¼ cup sliced and seeded green bell pepper

¼ cup sliced and seeded yellow bell pepper

¼ cup sliced and seeded red bell pepper

¼ cup sliced red onion

½ teaspoon freshly squeezed lime juice

2 tablespoons Stealthy Healthy Mayo (page 139)

8 gluten-free corn tortillas

Slice the plantain into ½-inch-thick coins and then quarter each coin. In a medium-size skillet, heat the olive oil over medium-high heat. Add the plantains and ⅛ teaspoon of salt and brown on all sides, about 5 minutes. Add 1 tablespoon of the water and cover. Continue to cook over medium-high heat until the water is absorbed and the plantains are tender.

In a small saucepan, mix the red beans with ⅛ teaspoon of salt and the garlic powder and cumin and warm just until heated. Set aside.

Place the peppers, onion, and remaining ½ tablespoon of water in a skillet and sprinkle with ⅛ teaspoon of salt. Cook over medium-high heat until the vegetables are tender, about 7 minutes. In a small bowl, mix together the lime juice and mayo to use as an accompaniment.

Warm the tortillas either in the oven or on a flat burner until toasted. Fill with the plantains, red beans, and vegetables and top with a dollop of lime mayo.

YIELD:

8 SERVINGS

PER SERVING:

174 CALORIES

2.2 G FAT

260 MG SODIUM

499 MG POTASSIUM

33.4 G CARBOHYDRATES

7 G PROTEIN

Sun-Dried Tomato Guacamole

Throwing some tomatoes into your guacamole adds a bit of color and oomph to the already decadent dip. This recipe takes that idea one step further by using sun-dried tomatoes, which are like little flavor bombs that also happen to be good sources of vitamins A and C, calcium, and iron. Seek out dried sun-dried tomatoes for this recipe, rather than the ones packed in oil. If you find they are too tough straight from the package, simply soak them for an hour or so and pat dry before chopping. Delicious served with fresh-cut veggies, such as celery, broccoli, and/or carrot sticks.

2 average-size ripe avocados, peeled and pitted

2 teaspoons freshly squeezed lime juice

¼ teaspoon salt, or a touch more to taste

1 tablespoon minced fresh chives

1 tablespoon minced fresh cilantro

2 large oil-free sun-dried tomatoes, chopped into very small pieces

Pinch of freshly ground black pepper

Place the avocados in a medium-size bowl. Using a fork or a small potato masher, gently mash the avocados until smooth, drizzling the lime juice and sprinkling the salt evenly into the avocados as you mash them. Fold in the chives, cilantro, and chopped sun-dried tomatoes and mix gently but thoroughly. Sprinkle with the black pepper. Store in an airtight container for up to 2 days in the refrigerator.

YIELD:

8 SERVINGS

PER SERVING:

107 CALORIES

9.8 G FAT

87 MG SODIUM

276 MG POTASSIUM

5.5 G CARBOHYDRATES

1.1 G PROTEIN

Superfresh Salsa

This salsa is great served with tortilla or veggie chips or as a flavorful topping for so many other dishes. Try it on pasta, baked potatoes, as a zesty stir-in to chili; the options are endless! If you prefer a milder salsa, remove and discard the seeds from the jalapeño before blending. Bell peppers are botanically considered fruits rather than vegetables and are an excellent source of carotenoids, which have been connected to reducing the risk of diseases, especially of the eye, and certain cancers.

2 cups coarsely chopped tomatoes

1 cup coarsely chopped and seeded bell peppers

⅓ cup fresh cilantro

4 scallions, chopped

1 jalapeño pepper, chopped

1 teaspoon salt

1 tablespoon cider vinegar

Place all the ingredients in a food processor and pulse briefly just until well combined and the veggies are in small pieces.

Alternatively, cut the tomatoes and bell peppers into small cubes and place in a bowl. Finely chop the cilantro, scallions, and jalapeño, and toss with the tomatoes and bell peppers. Add the salt and cider vinegar and toss to combine. Let rest for at least 30 minutes before serving.

YIELD:

8 SERVINGS

PER SERVING:

15 CALORIES

0.1 G FAT

295 MG SODIUM

160 MG POTASSIUM

3.2 G CARBOHYDRATES

0.7 G PROTEIN

Papaya Salad OF

This salad is a savory recipe featuring a sweet tropical fruit. For best results, let this rest for at least a few hours; I like the flavor best after the ingredients have time to really relax and enjoy each other's company. Papaya is rich in a variety of good stuff such as vitamin C, folate, and fiber. It also contains the enzyme papain, similar to the bromelain found in pineapple, which is helpful in healing bruising and injuries to the skin.

1 large papaya, peeled and cubed (about 2½ cups)

½ cup chopped fresh cilantro

¼ cup chopped fresh parsley

2 tablespoons freshly squeezed lime juice

½ teaspoon lime zest

1 clove garlic, minced

2 tablespoons chopped fresh chives

½ teaspoon salt

Place all the ingredients in a large bowl and toss lightly to combine. Cover and allow to rest for 30 minutes at room temperature and then transfer to the refrigerator to rest for at least 2 more hours, up to overnight. Serve cold.

YIELD:

6 SERVINGS

PER SERVING:

32 CALORIES

0.2 G FAT

201 MG SODIUM

153 MG POTASSIUM

8.2 G CARBOHYDRATES

0.5 G PROTEIN

Minted Watermelon Salad

Watermelon doesn't need much to make it taste truly outstanding, and mint does just the trick to take the common melon from "yum" to "yowza!" Like tomatoes, watermelon is high in lycopene, an important nutrient found in red-, orange-, and pink-hued foods. The lycopene content in watermelons is said to be higher when the fruit is allowed to ripen from whitish pink to dark pink. Make a big batch of this salad for a refreshing treat on a superhot day.

2 cups cubed and seeded watermelon (about 1-inch cubes)

Zest of 1 lemon (about 1 teaspoon)

½ teaspoon salt

1 tablespoon freshly squeezed lemon juice

2 tablespoons chopped fresh mint leaves

Place the watermelon in a medium-size bowl. Toss with the lemon zest, salt, and lemon juice. Fold in the chopped mint leaves. Let rest for 10 minutes before serving. Best if served chilled.

Store in an airtight container in the refrigerator for up to 3 days.

YIELD:

4 SERVINGS

PER SERVING:

25 CALORIES

0.1 G FAT

293 MG SODIUM

104 MG POTASSIUM

6.1 G CARBOHYDRATES

0.6 G PROTEIN

Kiwi Salad

There's no denying the allure of a simple fruit salad; the magic lies in the combination of fruits used. This salad features the dynamic duo of strawberry and kiwi, with an extra sweet touch from the mango and a slightly savory note from the fragrant Indian spice blend garam masala. To make a dish that travels well, reserve the sprinkling of the spices until just before serving so the color stays brilliant.

2 kiwis, peeled and cut into bite-size pieces

6 strawberries, sliced

½ cup chopped mango

1 tablespoon coconut cream (see page 9)

1 teaspoon freshly squeezed lemon juice

¼ teaspoon garam masala

½ teaspoon ground cinnamon

Place the kiwis, strawberries, and mango in a medium-size bowl. Toss with the coconut cream and lemon juice to coat.

In a very small bowl, mix the garam masala and cinnamon and sprinkle on the top of the fruit salad before serving. Enjoy within 2 days. Store in the refrigerator in an airtight container.

YIELD:

4 SERVINGS

PER SERVING:

56 CALORIES

1.2 G FAT

3 MG SODIUM

198 MG POTASSIUM

11.7 G CARBOHYDRATES

0.8 G PROTEIN

Dried Fruit Salad

This "fruit salad" is one of my staple recipes for trail mix, as it features a variety of fruits that make it taste much more like dessert than a healthy snack. You can certainly use other types of dried fruit in place of the ones listed, but I really like the flavor combo of the goji, mulberries, and golden raisins. Dried mulberries are available in white and black varieties and can be sourced at many natural foods and health food stores, as well as online. Like many berries, mulberries contain a few different nutrients that act as antioxidants, as well as are a great source of vitamin C (100 g contains 60% RDI) and iron (100 g contains 20% RDI). My husband and I like to share a bowl of Dried Fruit Salad when we're craving something sweet (and easy!).

½ cup goji berries

½ cup golden raisins

⅓ cup dried mulberries

½ cup sunflower seeds

¼ cup certified gluten-free rolled oats

¼ cup pepitas

Place all the ingredients in a bowl and toss well to combine. Store for up to 2 months in an airtight resalable container.

YIELD:

8 SERVINGS

PER SERVING:

141 CALORIES

6.3 G FAT

2 MG SODIUM

116 MG POTASSIUM

20.2 G CARBOHYDRATES

3.9 G PROTEIN

Chia pudding is brightened up with the light flavors of lemon and lime. Our body readily utilizes limonen, a compound found in limes and lemons, which is an antioxidant similar to the phenols found in green tea. Even though this pudding takes less than thirty minutes to come together, it keeps great in the fridge, so you can make this at night before going to sleep and wake up to a simple sunny breakfast.

¼ cup maple or coconut palm sugar

1 tablespoon freshly squeezed lemon juice

1 tablespoon freshly squeezed lime juice

½ teaspoon lemon zest

½ teaspoon lime zest

½ teaspoon pure vanilla extract

¼ cup white chia seeds

1 cup unsweetened almond milk

¼ cup coconut cream (optional; see page 9)

In a small bowl, dissolve the sugar in the lemon and lime juice. Mix in the rest of the ingredients, stirring well after each addition. Transfer to four small serving dishes and cover with plastic wrap. Place in the refrigerator and allow to rest for at least 30 minutes, or until the mixture has gelled. I enjoy eating this very cold, so I prefer to chill it about 2 hours before serving. Top each chia pudding with 1 tablespoon of coconut cream, if desired, for an extra-indulgent treat. Keeps for up to 4 days in an airtight container in the refrigerator.

YIELD:

4 SERVINGS

PER SERVING:

85 CALORIES

3.7 G FAT

23 MG SODIUM

119 MG POTASSIUM

13.3 G CARBOHYDRATES

3.8 G PROTEIN

WITH COCONUT CREAM TOPPING:

154 CALORIES

7.8 G FAT

26 MG SODIUM

159 MG POTASSIUM

16.2 G CARBOHYDRATES

5.7 G PROTEIN

Carrot Applesauce Muffins

Moist and tender, these muffins rely on the combo of carrots and applesauce for their texture and a bit of unrefined sweetness. The maple sugar truly adds a nice depth of flavor but another type of unrefined sugar, such as coconut palm, will also do.

2 medium-size carrots, shredded (about 1 cup)

¾ cup unsweetened applesauce

⅓ cup maple or coconut palm sugar

¾ teaspoon salt

1 tablespoon olive or coconut oil

1 cup chickpea flour

½ cup buckwheat flour

1½ teaspoons baking powder

½ teaspoon baking soda

¾ cup unsweetened almond milk

Preheat your oven to 350°F and line twelve standard-size muffin cups with paper liners. In a large bowl, mix together the carrots, applesauce, maple sugar, salt, and olive oil. Stir well to combine and then add the rest of the ingredients, stirring again to get rid of any lumps. Let the batter rest for 1 to 2 minutes and then divide evenly among the prepared muffin cups. Bake on the middle rack of the oven for 25 minutes, or until a knife inserted into the middle of a muffin comes out clean.

Store in an airtight container for up to 3 days.

YIELD:

12 SERVINGS

PER SERVING:

109 CALORIES

1.5 G FAT

223 MG SODIUM

309 MG POTASSIUM

20.5 G CARBOHYDRATES

4.5 G PROTEIN

This recipe is best made on a nonstick griddle or skillet, as it uses no oil in the recipe and lots of bananas. The nonstick surface will prevent the batter from sticking to the cooking surface. Alternatively, you can use a bit of cooking oil on a regular skillet to make these (note that the pancakes will no longer be oil free); just avoid cast iron, as the batter will most likely stick to this type of pan.

3 small very ripe bananas, peeled

¾ cup superfine brown rice flour

1 teaspoon baking powder

2 tablespoons flaxseed meal

½ teaspoon salt

1 teaspoon ground cinnamon

1 cup unsweetened almond milk

Heat a griddle to 325° to 350°F. In a medium-size bowl, mash the bananas completely and stir in the brown rice flour, baking powder, flaxseed meal, salt, and cinnamon. Mix in the almond milk, using a whisk, and stir until no lumps remain in the batter. Place about ¼ cup of batter on the hot griddle, using the back of a spoon to gently smooth it into a 4-inch circle. Repeat to add more pancakes to the griddle, allowing room between them for easy flipping. Let cook for about 2 minutes, or until the tops are bubbly and the pancakes easily release from the griddle with a flat spatula. Do not flip too soon or you will ruin the pancakes. Flip and cook for an additional 1 to 2 minutes, or until both sides are golden. Repeat with the remaining batter. Let cool briefly and then enjoy.

YIELD:

8 SERVINGS

PER SERVING:

74 CALORIES

1.3 G FAT

160 MG SODIUM

275 MG POTASSIUM

14.6 G CARBOHYDRATES

2.2 G PROTEIN

Cinnamon Plum Streusel

Use barely ripe plums for the best texture and sweetness in this comforting dessert, which has a crispy oat crumble topping and soft, sweet, fragrant filling. Research suggests that plums have the ability to help the body utilize iron more efficiently by helping with absorption, which could be due to their vitamin C content.

3 tablespoons almond meal

2 plums, pitted and thinly sliced

½ cup chickpea flour

½ teaspoon baking powder

¼ teaspoon salt

1 teaspoon ground cinnamon, plus more for dusting

1 tablespoon pure maple syrup, plus more (about 1 teaspoon) for sprinkling

¼ cup water

¼ cup certified gluten-free rolled oats

Preheat your oven to 375°F and line an 8-inch square pan with parchment paper. Sprinkle the bottom of the pan with the almond meal. Cover the almond meal evenly with the plum slices, taking care not to overlap the plums.

In a small bowl, whisk together the chickpea flour, baking powder, salt, and cinnamon. Mix in the maple syrup and water and whisk until very smooth. Drizzle the batter evenly over the plums. Sprinkle with the oats and then top the oats with a sprinkle of cinnamon and a touch of maple syrup. Bake for 25 minutes, or until the plums are very tender. Let cool briefly before enjoying. Best if eaten the same day as prepared.

YIELD:

6 SERVINGS

PER SERVING:

97 CALORIES

2.5 G FAT

102 MG SODIUM

201 MG POTASSIUM

15.7 G CARBOHYDRATES

4 G PROTEIN

Roasted Pears with Walnuts

A beautiful recipe to make for a special occasion, or to make a simple occasion more special. Any variety of pears can be used, but make sure they are ripe for perfectly roasted pears, rather than overly hard or too mushy. When a pear is perfectly ripe, the flesh will give ever so slightly when pressed or squeezed gently.

2 pears, any variety

⅓ cup crushed walnuts

½ teaspoon ground cinnamon

2 tablespoons coconut palm or maple sugar

2 tablespoons pure maple or agave syrup

Pinch of salt

Preheat your oven to 350°F and line a small baking dish with parchment paper. Cut the pears in half from top to bottom. Remove the pear seeds, using a small spoon or melon scooper, so that you create a scooped depression in each pear half. Fill the depressions with crushed walnuts and place the pears, stuffing side up, snugly side by side in the baking dish. Sprinkle the pears evenly with the cinnamon and coconut palm sugar and then drizzle with the maple syrup. Sprinkle a touch of salt onto each pear and bake for 40 to 45 minutes, until the pears are tender and fragrant. Enjoy immediately.

YIELD:

4 SERVINGS

PER SERVING:

174 CALORIES

6.3 G FAT

90 MG SODIUM

197 MG POTASSIUM

29.9 G CARBOHYDRATES

2.9 G PROTEIN

Chocolate Gooseberry Pudding

Gooseberries are seasonal delicacies, available May through August and at their peak in July. They taste a little bit like tart grapes and look a little like grapes, too, but they also have a wispy, papery covering, much like a lantern. Gooseberries, related to currants, are high in fiber and come in a variety of colors, including red, green, and yellow. They are known to contain GLA (gamma-linolenic acid), an omega-6 fatty acid linked to better kidney, nerve, and reproductive health. I like to play off gooseberries' sour flavor profile by adding these fruits to sweet treats, such as this decadent chocolate pudding.

1 cup gooseberries

⅔ cup unrefined sugar, such as coconut palm or maple

1½ cups unsweetened almond milk

1 teaspoon pure vanilla extract

¼ teaspoon salt

2 tablespoons superfine brown rice flour

3 tablespoons chickpea flour

⅓ cup water

1 tablespoon unsweetened cocoa powder

Preheat your oven to 400°F. Line a large baking sheet with parchment paper. Peel the papery covering from the gooseberries and rinse the berries well to remove any stickiness. Arrange the berries on the prepared baking sheet and bake for 20 minutes.

Over medium heat, stir together the unrefined sugar, almond milk, vanilla extract, and salt. In a small bowl, whisk together the superfine brown rice flour, chickpea flour, and water until no lumps remain. Gradually whisk the flour mixture into the heated almond milk and stir constantly while continuing to heat over medium heat. Whisk in the cocoa powder and keep cooking until thickened, 5 to 7 minutes. Stir in the roasted gooseberries.

Transfer to four small heatproof containers and let cool at room temperature for about 20 minutes. Transfer to the refrigerator and chill until cold.

YIELD:

4 SERVINGS

PER SERVING:

280 CALORIES

2.7 G FAT

257 MG SODIUM

304 MG POTASSIUM

59.4 G CARBOHYDRATES

7.3 G PROTEIN

Caramel Apple Parfaits

These cute parfaits are a wonderful way to enjoy apples. Lightly spiced with cinnamon, this healthy parfait makes an indulgent dessert. To easily toast the walnuts or pecans, simply spread the nuts in an even layer on an ungreased baking sheet. Preheat your oven to 400°F and then bake for 7 minutes, or until fragrant.

1 recipe Simple Cashew Cream (page 135)

1 teaspoon ground cinnamon

¼ teaspoon freshly grated nutmeg

⅛ teaspoon ground cloves

1 tablespoon pure maple syrup

FOR THE CARAMEL APPLE LAYER

1 medium-size apple, skin on, cored and cubed into ½-inch pieces

5 Medjool dates, pitted

⅓ cup plus ¼ cup water

1 teaspoon pure vanilla extract

¼ teaspoon salt

FOR THE CRUMBLE

½ cup crushed walnuts or pecans, toasted

1 teaspoon ground cinnamon

⅛ teaspoon salt

In a medium-size bowl, whisk together the cashew cream, cinnamon, nutmeg, cloves, and maple syrup.

Make the caramel apple layer: Place the cubed apples and dates in a small saucepan along with ⅓ cup of the water. Cook over medium heat until the fruit is softened, 7 to 10 minutes, stirring often. Drain and transfer to a blender and blend along with the remaining ¼ cup of water and the vanilla extract and salt.

Make the crumble: Pulse the toasted walnuts, cinnamon, and salt in a food processor just until crumbly.

Assemble the parfaits by layering the spiced cashew cream, then the caramel apples, then the walnut crumble, and finally topping with more cashew cream. Serve chilled.

YIELD:

4 SERVINGS

PER SERVING:

300 CALORIES

20 G FAT

226 MG SODIUM

277 MG POTASSIUM

31.1 G CARBOHYDRATES

8 G PROTEIN

Hunky Monkey Ice Cream

This recipe is much like the famous Ben and Jerry's flavor, except that the delicious "ice cream" base is made with only bananas. Frozen bananas have the ability to magically transform into the same texture as hand-dipped ice cream when blended. Add cacao nibs for a delicious dark chocolate flavor and crunchy walnuts for a decadent treat!

6 bananas, peeled and frozen

1 teaspoon pure vanilla extract

¼ cup cacao nibs

½ cup walnuts, finely chopped

Place the frozen bananas in a food processor and blend. This is easiest to do if you pulse, scrape, pulse, scrape, and keep repeating until the bananas become crumbly or chopped into pea-size pieces. At this point, add the vanilla extract and continue to blend just until smooth. The mixture will eventually have a texture like that of thick ice cream. Transfer to a large bowl and fold in the cacao nibs and walnuts. The texture of this ice cream is best if eaten immediately (it melts just like ice cream, too!), but you can also freeze any leftovers in a flexible airtight container and allow to thaw or soften about 10 minutes before serving.

YIELD:

8 SERVINGS

PER SERVING:

140 CALORIES

5.4 G FAT

1 MG SODIUM

358 MG POTASSIUM

22.5 G CARBOHYDRATES

3.2 G PROTEIN

Blueberries and Cream Mousse

Simply sweet, this fluffy mousse can be whipped up whenever the craving strikes. You'll love how bold this easy dessert both tastes and looks! With a bright purple color and blast of fresh blueberry flavor, and a nice dose of protein from the tofu, this treat is one you'll find yourself craving again and again.

2 cups blueberries

12.3 ounces light firm silken tofu

4 large Medjool dates, pitted

1½ tablespoons freshly squeezed lemon juice

Place all the ingredients in a blender or small food processor and blend until very smooth, stopping and scraping down the sides of the blender container or processor bowl as needed. Place in serving dishes or a resealable airtight container and chill for 1 hour in the refrigerator to firm. Enjoy cold.

YIELD:

4 SERVINGS

PER SERVING:

122 CALORIES

1 G FAT

76 MG SODIUM

118 MG POTASSIUM

23.8 G CARBOHYDRATES

6.7 G PROTEIN

Cantaloupe Mango Sorbet

Cantaloupe is high in both vitamins A and C and potassium, while mango boasts a good amount of vitamin B_6, folate, and copper. Combined, they make an irresistible, brightly flavored sorbet. If you happen to have a lot of fruit on hand and you'd like to make enough to share with friends, simply double or triple the batch.

1 cup cubed cantaloupe

1 cup cubed mango

⅓ cup pure maple syrup

3 Medjool dates, pitted

Place all the ingredients in a blender and blend until very smooth. Transfer to the bowl of an ice-cream maker and process according to the manufacturer's instructions. Alternatively, you can simply pour the mixture into a flexible plastic container once you have blended the mixture and place in the freezer. Every 20 minutes, stir using a whisk, until well blended and frozen throughout. Store in an airtight container in the freezer for up to 1 month.

YIELD:

1 PINT/4 SERVINGS

PER SERVING:

145 CALORIES

0.2 G FAT

11 MG SODIUM

286 MG POTASSIUM

36.8 G CARBOHYDRATES

0.9 G PROTEIN

Cardamom Orange Ice

This zesty, easy crushed ice makes an oh-so-refreshing dessert on a hot day. Any type of orange juice will work beautifully in this recipe; however, I am quite partial to mandarin oranges due to their extra fragrant and sweet juice.

2 cups freshly squeezed orange juice

1½ teaspoons pure vanilla extract

½ teaspoon ground cardamom

1 teaspoon freshly squeezed lemon juice

In a medium-size bowl, whisk together all the ingredients until very well combined. Make sure there is adequate room in your freezer for a small metal cake pan (8 or 9 inches wide) to lie flat. Pour the orange juice mixture into the pan and cover with plastic wrap. Place in the freezer and freeze for 5 hours, or until completely frozen solid. Using a fork, scrape the mixture quickly to form a fluffy frozen ice. Try not to overdo it with the scraping as it will turn to a slushy-like mixture. Quickly transfer the fluffy ice to an airtight resealable container. Store in the freezer for up to 2 months.

YIELD:

4 SERVINGS

PER SERVING:

62 CALORIES

0.3 G FAT

1 MG SODIUM

255 MG POTASSIUM

13.3 G CARBOHYDRATES

0.9 G PROTEIN

Beyond Good BBQ Sauce

This tasty BBQ sauce rivals the store-bought stuff and contains no sketchy ingredients. Vegan Worcestershire sauce really takes the flavor of this sauce to the next level, so be sure to include it; you can generally find this ingredient in natural food stores, online, or even in natural foods sections of many grocery chains. Use this recipe wherever you normally would use BBQ sauce: grilled tofu, as an alternative pizza sauce, or as a dipping sauce for my Popcorn Tofu (page 145).

1 (6-ounce) can tomato paste

½ cup water

1 tablespoon cider vinegar

2 teaspoons pure maple syrup

2 tablespoons raspberry, strawberry, or grape preserves (no added sugar)

1 teaspoon smoked paprika

2 cloves garlic, pressed or finely minced

1 teaspoon ground chili seasoning

2 teaspoons vegan Worcestershire sauce

½ teaspoon mustard powder

½ teaspoon celery salt

⅛ to ½ teaspoon salt

Combine all the ingredients, except the salt, in a small saucepan and stir well, using a fork or small whisk. Add salt to taste, if desired. Simmer over medium-low heat for 10 to 15 minutes, stirring often. Store in an airtight container in the refrigerator for up to 1 week.

YIELD:

8 SERVINGS

PER SERVING:

40 CALORIES

0.2 G FAT

48 MG SODIUM

232 MG POTASSIUM

9.3 G CARBOHYDRATES

1.1 G PROTEIN

Raspberry Vinaigrette

Bright both in flavor and in color, this dressing is lighter than most traditional vinaigrettes as it doesn't contain oil, but fresh raspberries instead. Raspberries are some of the world's most popular berries and are chock-full of antioxidants and anti-inflammatory phytonutrients, as well as vitamin C, manganese, and fiber. Since they are quite perishable, you should try to use raspberries within one to two days of purchasing, and this is a great recipe for using them up quickly.

1 cup fresh raspberries

¼ cup raw cider vinegar, such as Bragg's

1 tablespoon freshly squeezed lemon juice

⅛ teaspoon salt

1 large Medjool date, pitted

¼ cup water

Rinse the raspberries and place along with the cider vinegar, lemon juice, salt, Medjool date, and water in a blender and blend until very smooth. Store the dressing in an airtight container for up to 2 weeks in the refrigerator. Makes about 1½ cups.

YIELD:

12 SERVINGS

PER SERVING:

9 CALORIES

0.1 G FAT

24 MG SODIUM

21 MG POTASSIUM

1.9 G CARBOHYDRATES

0.2 G PROTEIN

ACV Fizz

ACV stands for "apple cider vinegar," and we're not just talking about any ol' apple cider vinegar. Seek out raw apple cider vinegars, such as Bragg's, which include the "mother," or the strands of enzymes, proteins, and beneficial bacteria. This type of ACV is said to be nutritionally superior to the more processed or distilled varieties. This zippy beverage includes probiotics from the ACV and vitamin C from the lemon juice. You can easily make this a comforting hot tea by subbing out the seltzer for almost-boiling water instead. Stir and enjoy!

Juice of 1 lemon (about 2 tablespoons)

2 tablespoons unfiltered raw apple cider vinegar

1 tablespoon maple sugar, or a dash of stevia

1 cup seltzer water

Mix the lemon juice, apple cider vinegar, and maple sugar together until well blended. Add the seltzer water and stir gently. Enjoy immediately.

YIELD:

1 SERVING

PER SERVING:

63 CALORIES

0.3 G FAT

4 MG SODIUM

162 MG POTASSIUM

16.3 G CARBOHYDRATES

0.9 G PROTEIN

Rosemary Cucumber Cooler

Don't fall for the hype of vitamin waters that you can find in many gas stations and beverage coolers; opt for the real stuff and drink infused water instead! When you infuse water by adding chopped whole fruits and vegetables, you are allowing some nutrients from the fruits and veggies to actually seep into the water itself, giving it not only a nice burst of refreshing flavor, but a nutritional boost as well! Have a pitcher of this refreshing beverage on hand for days when you want to truly quench your thirst. The crisp taste of cucumber in this cooler is lightly scented with rosemary and lemon. Use this recipe as a simple base and experiment with various flavors, such as strawberry, parsley, lime, apple, carrot—the options are truly endless.

1 gallon filtered water

1 cucumber, sliced

1 lemon, sliced

1 (6-inch) sprig
    rosemary

Pour the filtered water into a large glass jar or pitcher. Add the cucumber slices, lemon slices, and rosemary sprig. Cover and chill for at least 1 hour and up to 2 days. Strain and enjoy.

YIELD:

12 SERVINGS

PER SERVING:

4 CALORIES

0 G FAT

10 MG SODIUM

40 MG POTASSIUM

0.9 G
CARBOHYDRATES

0.2 G PROTEIN

CHAPTER 4

NUTS & SEEDS

Full of flavor and super filling, nuts and seeds are an important part of a well-balanced diet, as they deliver protein, good fats, and fiber in a compact little container. You only need a few nuts and seeds a day to reap their nutritional benefits, and the recipes featured on the following pages highlight the many ways to enjoy them—whether they take a starring role for flavor and crunch or they're in the background for extra creaminess. From filling mains, such as the Pad Thai Soba Noodles (page 112) to simple snacks, such as the Flax and Chia Garlic Crackers (page 116), this chapter shows you how to make the very most out of nuts and seeds.

Insanely Addictive Queso

I've long had a love-hate relationship with queso—starting way back in grade school, when I'd hang out at the local skating rink, chowing down on nachos covered in the nuclear-colored goo before meeting a boy to skate the moonlight skate. Memories aside, that cheesy goop didn't exactly taste good, and I never really liked queso—until I discovered cashew-based queso. It blows that other stuff away on flavor, and it's as easy to prepare as it is to gobble up. For even quicker and easier queso, have the cashews soaked and ready to go before beginning.

2 cups raw cashews, soaked in water for 1 hour and drained

1 orange bell pepper, seeded

1 cup unsweetened almond milk, plus more to thin

1⅛ teaspoons salt

2 teaspoons chili powder

⅓ cup nutritional yeast flakes

Place the soaked cashews, bell pepper, and unsweetened almond milk in a high-speed blender and blend until almost completely mixed; there will still be granules of cashew in the mix. Add the salt, chili powder, and nutritional yeast flakes and continue to blend, stopping and stirring often, until totally smooth and creamy, adding up to 2 teaspoons of additional almond milk to thin. You can also use a food processor to blend (about 5 minutes), but I recommend a blender for ultimate smoothness.

Once blended, you can heat the queso in a small saucepan, although I like it served at room temperature. Serve with tortilla chips or sliced veggies. Also delicious as a topper for nachos.

YIELD:

10 SERVINGS

PER SERVING:

185 CALORIES

13.5 G FAT

295 G SODIUM

331 MG POTASSIUM

12.4 G CARBOHYDRATES

6.9 G PROTEIN

Pad Thai Soba Noodles

For an easy meal that will fill you up and never let you down, try these soba noodles. Delicately spiced and seriously delicious, they are flavored with ingredients inspired by Thailand. Take care to check the ingredients on the soba noodles to make sure they are 100 percent buckwheat, as some brands also include wheat flour as an ingredient. (Bonus! 100 percent buckwheat noodles are also fat-free). I've had good luck sourcing 100 percent buckwheat noodles at Asian markets and online.

½ to 1 teaspoon sesame or olive oil

1 bell pepper, any color, seeded and diced

½ onion, diced

6 cremini mushrooms, sliced

1 teaspoon grated fresh ginger

½ teaspoon salt

8 ounces 100 percent buckwheat soba noodles

½ teaspoon gluten-free soy sauce

1 recipe Thai Peanut Dressing (page 113)

¼ cup sliced scallions

In a large skillet, heat the oil over medium-high heat and add the bell pepper, onion, mushrooms, and grated ginger. Sprinkle evenly with the salt and sauté until the onion is translucent, 5 to 7 minutes.

Cook the buckwheat noodles according to the package directions and toss with the soy sauce to evenly distribute. Let rest for 2 minutes, then coat with the Thai Peanut Dressing. Top with the sautéed vegetables and then the scallions. Serve immediately.

YIELD:

6 SERVINGS

PER SERVING:

300 CALORIES

14.4 G FAT

728 MG SODIUM

285 MG POTASSIUM

39.9 G CARBOHYDRATES

12.6 G PROTEIN

Thai Peanut Dressing

The spicy level is optional in this peanutty dressing; leave the cayenne out completely for a mild sauce. Although it's fabulous as a salad topper, this recipe also doubles as a delicious sauce for pasta (see Pad Thai Soba Noodles, page 112).

½ cup crunchy or smooth peanut butter, no sugar or oils added

¼ cup water

1 cup light canned coconut milk

½ small clove garlic

2 teaspoons gluten-free soy sauce

½ tablespoon freshly squeezed lime juice

2 Medjool dates, pitted, or 2 tablespoons pure maple syrup

½ teaspoon sweet paprika

½ teaspoon cayenne powder, or to taste

Place all the ingredients in a blender and blend on high speed until smooth, stopping and scraping down the sides of the blender container as needed. Store in an airtight container in the refrigerator for up to 1 week.

YIELD:

20 SERVINGS

PER SERVING:

53 CALORIES

3.9 G FAT

28 MG SODIUM

44 MG POTASSIUM

3.9 G CARBOHYDRATES

2.0 G PROTEIN

Pecan-Stuffed Okra

A fun dish to serve at parties and potlucks, okra pods are the perfect vehicle for an irresistible pecan filling. The key here is to thoroughly dry the okra pods after washing, so that the okra does not end up sticky, but instead crispy and just slightly tender.

20 okra pods

1 cup finely chopped pecans

1 clove garlic, minced

1 large shallot, minced

½ teaspoon salt

1 teaspoon ground cumin

¼ teaspoon ground coriander

1 teaspoon olive oil

Preheat your oven to 425°F and line a baking sheet with parchment paper or a silicone mat. Wash the okra pods and dry very thoroughly with a clean towel. Carefully slice just the top off the pods and then slice down the middle of each pod lengthwise, but not cutting all the way through, so that you end up with okra pods that resemble little boats. In a medium-size bowl, combine the pecans, garlic, shallot, salt, cumin, and coriander until well mixed. Using a small spoon, stuff the pods with the filling as best you can, allowing some to heap over the top. Place the stuffed pods side by side on the prepared baking sheet and lightly drizzle with the olive oil. Bake for 15 to 17 minutes, until fragrant and tender.

YIELD:

6 SERVINGS

PER SERVING:

148 CALORIES

12.4 G FAT

200 MG SODIUM

326 MG POTASSIUM

8.9 G CARBOHYDRATES

3.5 G PROTEIN

Walnut Eggplant Dip

This dip is much like baba ghanoush, but with the added earthy flavor of walnuts. It is delicious served simply with raw zucchini slices, but it also makes a fab sandwich or collard wrap spread or pizza topping (used like a sauce).

1 standard-size eggplant

1 shallot

1 clove garlic

1 tablespoon plus 2 teaspoons freshly squeezed lemon juice

Salt

1 cup walnuts

1 teaspoon fresh thyme leaves

Preheat your oven to 400°F. Line a cookie sheet with parchment paper and slice the eggplant in half. Place the eggplant, cut side up, on the prepared cookie sheet along with the shallot and garlic clove. Drizzle with 2 teaspoons of the lemon juice and sprinkle with ⅛ teaspoon of salt. Cover lightly with foil and bake for 45 to 50 minutes. Let cool for about 15 minutes.

Scoop the eggplant flesh from the skin and place in a food processor along with the roasted shallot and garlic. Add the walnuts, the thyme, the 1 tablespoon of lemon juice, and ½ teaspoon of salt. Blend well until the mixture is very smooth, about 5 minutes, stopping and scraping down the sides of the bowl as needed. Add additional salt, up to ¼ teaspoon more, if desired. Store the dip in an airtight container for up to 1 week in the refrigerator.

YIELD:

6 SERVINGS

PER SERVING:

151 CALORIES

12.5 G FAT

197 MG SODIUM

298 MG POTASSIUM

7.2 G CARBOHYDRATES

5.9 G PROTEIN

Flax and Chia Garlic Crackers

Made from carrot, onion, garlic, and seeds, these crispy, crunchy little crackers will surprise you with their full flavor. Every time I make a batch of these I end up snacking on them all throughout the day, as they are incredibly irresistible crackers that keep me going back for more.

½ cup whole flaxseeds

½ cup whole chia seeds

1 small carrot, cut into 1-inch pieces

3 cloves garlic

1 small onion, peeled and chopped

1 teaspoon salt

Preheat your oven to 250°F and cover a large baking sheet with parchment paper. Place all the ingredients in a food processor and blend until the onion and carrot are completely pureed and the mixture is very well combined (the seeds will remain whole and the mixture should be thick enough to roll. If it is too thin, simply add more flax and chia until workable). Spread the mixture on the prepared baking sheet by placing another sheet of parchment on top of the mixture; using your hands, press down and outward gently to spread into a thin layer (about ⅛ inch thick). Carefully peel off the top layer of parchment and bake on the middle rack of the oven for 45 minutes, or until crispy and golden brown.

Let cool completely and then break into crackers. Store in an airtight container for up to 1 week.

YIELD:

5 SERVINGS

PER SERVING:

118 CALORIES

7.5 G FAT

476 MG SODIUM

230 MG POTASSIUM

10.9 G CARBOHYDRATES

4.8 G PROTEIN

Simple Soft and Chewy Granola Bars

Granola bars pack a good bit of healthy fats and protein to satisfy hunger (and an occasional sweet tooth). I tend to be happiest when I have a week's worth of these bars on hand, so I can grab one and go whenever a craving for something sweet and salty strikes. Feel free to sub peanut butter or sunflower seed butter for the almond butter.

2 tablespoons ground chia seeds

2 tablespoons water

2½ cups certified gluten-free rolled oats

½ cup hemp hearts

1 teaspoon salt

1 teaspoon ground cinnamon

½ cup pure maple or agave syrup

¼ cup creamy almond butter

¼ cup almond meal

Coconut oil, for pressing

Preheat your oven to 350°F. Line an 8-inch square pan with parchment paper. In a small bowl, mix together the ground chia seeds with the water and allow the mixture to rest until gelled, about 5 minutes.

In a large mixing bowl, combine the oats, hemp hearts, salt, and cinnamon. Mix in the prepared chia seed gel, maple syrup, and almond butter. I find this easiest to do with clean hands. Once you have mixed in the ingredients until they are well incorporated, stir in the almond meal. Spread the mixture on the prepared pan and then press down firmly with lightly coconut-oiled hands. Bake for 20 minutes, or until golden brown and fragrant. While still hot, use a flat-edged spatula to cut into bars. Let cool completely, remove from the pan, and enjoy!

YIELD:

10 BARS

PER BAR:

214 CALORIES

9.4 G FAT

264 MG SODIUM

264 MG POTASSIUM

26.8 G CARBOHYDRATES

7.3 G PROTEIN

Chewy Cherry Chia Bars

Chia seeds are a good source of calcium, iron, and fiber. Great for a midday snack or as a light breakfast on the go, or for when you need a delicious nutritious bite without a lot of fuss. These chia bars are similar to Larabars: slightly soft, sticky, and super portable! I like to double this recipe and send a batch with my husband to work, so he has healthy treats that'll last all week.

1 cup raw cashews

1 cup certified gluten-free rolled oats

2 tablespoons chia seeds

½ teaspoon salt

⅔ cup dried cherries (no sugar added)

10 to 12 Medjool dates, pitted

Place the cashews, oats, chia seeds, salt, and dried cherries in a food processor and pulse until very crumbly and well blended. Add the dates one at a time, pulsing between additions, until the mixture sticks together easily when pinched. Depending on the size and softness of your dates, you may need to add more or less, but around ten should allow it to come together easily.

Once the mixture easily comes together, place in an 8-inch square baking pan and press down very firmly using a flat-edged spatula. Cut into bars, place in an airtight container with the bars separated by parchment paper, and enjoy for up to 1 week. Alternatively, roll the mixture into 1-inch balls and store for up to 1 week in an airtight container.

YIELD:

16 SERVINGS

PER SERVING:

151 CALORIES

4.7 G FAT

79 G SODIUM

151 MG POTASSIUM

26.7 G CARBOHYDRATES

2.7 G PROTEIN

Cocoa Carob Bars

These decadent morsels taste so much like an indulgent treat, you'll hardly notice that they're healthy! Carob is full of calcium, selenium, and polyphenols, which are powerful antioxidants. But if you don't have carob flour on hand, additional cocoa powder can be subbed in its place.

2 cups raw cashews

½ cup raw pecans

2 tablespoons carob flour

2 tablespoons cocoa powder

12 Medjool dates, pitted

1 teaspoon pure vanilla extract

⅛ teaspoon salt

Place the cashews and pecans in a food processor and blend until evenly crumbly. Add the carob flour and cocoa powder and blend until well combined. One by one, add the dates, pulsing well between each addition. Blend (on high speed if possible) until the dates and nuts combine into a fine crumble that's easy to squeeze into shape between your fingertips. Add the vanilla extract and salt and blend evenly.

Cover the bottom of an 8-inch square baking pan with plastic wrap. Transfer the mixture from the food processor to the prepared pan and press down firmly and evenly until the mixture is packed down tightly. Cut into bars and enjoy.

YIELD:

16 SERVINGS

PER SERVING:

183 CALORIES

14.3 G FAT

23 MG SODIUM

185 MG POTASSIUM

13 G CARBOHYDRATES

3.9 G PROTEIN

Vanilla Almond Granola

It may sound silly, but this is my favorite recipe in this entire book. I blame it on my obsession with various flavored granolas that kept me fueled when I was growing up, and though I loved vanilla almond flavor the best, it always proved to be somewhat elusive. Nowadays, it's even harder to find a decent granola that's not only great tasting, but also gluten free. This one fits the bill, and it's super simple to make!

2 cups certified gluten-free rolled oats

½ cup almond meal

½ cup sliced almonds

About ½ teaspoon vanilla seeds (from 1 vanilla bean pod, scraped), or 1½ teaspoons pure vanilla extract

2 tablespoons almond oil (or other cooking oil)

½ cup pure maple syrup

¼ teaspoon salt

Preheat your oven to 375°F and line a large baking sheet with parchment paper or a silicone mat.

Place the oats, almond meal, and sliced almonds in a large bowl and toss gently to combine. In a separate, smaller bowl, mix together the vanilla beans or extract, almond oil, maple syrup, and salt. Toss with the oat mixture to coat. Spread into an even layer on the prepared cookie sheet. Bake for 14 minutes. Stir gently, using a spatula, and bake for 5 more minutes, or until golden brown. Watch carefully during the last 5 minutes so as not to burn the granola. Let cool completely before enjoying. Store in an airtight container for up to 2 weeks.

YIELD:

10 SERVINGS

PER SERVING:

181 CALORIES

8.7 G FAT

60 MG SODIUM

102 MG POTASSIUM

23.4 G CARBOHYDRATES

4 G PROTEIN

Nutty Butter Cookies

These craveworthy no-bake cookies are such a treat and taste a lot like peanut butter cookies, but without all the added oil. Peanut flour—sometimes called "peanut powder"—can be found in most supermarkets, usually in the gluten-free flour section or near the peanut butter. If your grocery store doesn't carry it, it is also available online. While testing these cookies, my husband and I enjoyed several batches, and we arrived at a recipe that we think is spot on. We also discovered that they make a perfect snack for late-night movie streaming . . .

1 cup raw cashews

1 cup macadamia nuts

¼ cup plus 2 tablespoons peanut flour

10 to 11 Medjool dates, pitted

½ teaspoon salt

In a food processor, combine the raw cashews, macadamia nuts and ¼ cup of peanut flour and blend until rather crumbly, stopping and scraping down the sides of the bowl as needed until coarse crumbles form. Add eight of the Medjool dates, one at a time, and blend until the fine crumbles are formed—about the texture of almond meal. Sprinkle in the salt and pulse well to combine, again stopping and scraping the sides of the bowl as needed. Sprinkle in the 2 remaining tablespoons of peanut flour and add two or three more dates. Blend until the mixture clumps together evenly, adding one more date if needed to make the dough come together. Shape into 1½-inch balls and flatten into cookie shapes. Store in an airtight container for up to 1 week, or in the refrigerator for up to 3 weeks.

YIELD:

20 SERVINGS

PER SERVING:

213 CALORIES

8.3 G FAT

62 MG SODIUM

78 MG POTASSIUM

35.5 G CARBOHYDRATES

3.7 G PROTEIN

Chocolate-Covered Hemp Cookies

These soft and sweet cookies have a toasted nutty flavor from the hemp hearts and cashews and are topped with deep, dark chocolate. Freeze these cookies after baking for a quick, delicious, and healthy treat anytime a chocolate craving strikes.

1 cup raw cashews

¼ cup hemp hearts

2 tablespoons cacao nibs

7 Medjool dates, pitted

¼ teaspoon salt

2 teaspoons pure vanilla extract

1½ teaspoons ground chia seeds

1 tablespoon water

1 cup Too Good for You to Be True Chocolate (page 128)

Preheat your oven to 300°F. Line a cookie sheet with parchment paper.

Place the cashews, hemp hearts, cacao nibs, and dates in a food processor. Pulse until evenly crumbly and finely ground so that the mixture sticks together easily. In a small bowl, combine the salt, vanilla extract, ground chia seeds, and water and let rest for 5 minutes, until gelled.

Transfer the cashew mixture to a large bowl and mix well with the prepared chia seed mixture. Pat the dough into a disk and place between two sheets of plastic wrap. Roll to ¼ inch thick and cut out, using your favorite shaped cookie cutters. Transfer to the prepared cookie sheet and bake for 25 minutes.

Arrange an even layer of the chocolate on top of the cookies right when they get out of the oven and let rest 5 minutes. Use the back of a spoon to evenly spread the chocolate on the cookies. Chill briefly in the refrigerator until the chocolate has set.

YIELD:

20 SERVINGS

PER SERVING:

134 CALORIES

10.8 G FAT

33 MG SODIUM

76 MG POTASSIUM

7 G CARBOHYDRATES

3 G PROTEIN

Caramel Pepita Cookies

A sweet treat made from pumpkin seeds and Medjool dates, loaded with iron, protein, and fiber, these caramel-flavored cookies are a perfect excuse to indulge in dessert. Bonus: no cooking necessary!

1 cup pepitas

10 to 11 small Medjool dates, pitted

2 tablespoons unsalted unsweetened almond butter

1 teaspoon pure vanilla extract

In a food processor, pulse the pepitas, 10 dates, and the almond butter and vanilla extract until crumbly. Scrape down the sides of the bowl and continue to process until very well chopped, so that the mixture easily comes together into a compact ball once squeezed. Add one more date if the mixture still seems too crumbly after 2 minutes of blending. Squeeze into 1-inch balls and flatten slightly into cookies. Store in an airtight container for up to 1 week.

YIELD:

10 SERVINGS

PER SERVING:

95 CALORIES

8.1 G FAT

2 MG SODIUM

25 MG POTASSIUM

3 G CARBOHYDRATES

4.1 G PROTEIN

Chocolate Cheesecake

Dark and decadent, this cheesecake is made with cashews instead of cream cheese and makes a perfect centerpiece to a happy, healthy celebration such as a birthday or a wedding anniversary. You can use a larger springform pan in place of the 6-inch pan, but keep in mind that the pie will be shorter in height the wider the diameter of the pan.

FOR THE CRUST

2 tablespoons almond meal

1 tablespoon unsweetened cocoa powder

1 tablespoon maple or coconut palm sugar

FOR THE FILLING

2½ cups raw cashews, soaked in water for 4 hours and drained

½ cup plus 2 tablespoons coconut oil

10 Medjool dates, pitted

¼ cup freshly squeezed lemon juice

½ teaspoon salt

½ cup water

¼ cup unsweetened cocoa powder

In a small bowl, whisk together the crust ingredients and sprinkle in an even layer over the bottom of a 6-inch springform pan.

In the bowl of a food processor, blend the filling ingredients until very smooth, about 7 minutes, stopping and scraping down the sides of the bowl often. Pour the filling on top of the crust and use a flat-edged spatula to make the filling even on top. Cover with foil (do not let the foil touch the filling) and freeze for 6 hours. Thaw in the refrigerator for 1 to 2 hours, and then release the springform rim, slice, and serve.

YIELD:

12 SERVINGS

PER SERVING:

280 CALORIES

20 G FAT

100 MG SODIUM

210 MG POTASSIUM

21 G CARBOHYDRATES

4.3 G PROTEIN

Chocolate Gelato

I put this recipe in the seeds chapter because the primary flavor in this delicious dessert comes from cocoa beans (which are actually dried fermented seeds of the cacao tree). The base is made from avocado, which gives it an exceptionally silky-smooth texture, and coconut milk. Sweetened with maple syrup and dates, this seductively sweet concoction is just begging for you to indulge. For an extra "seedy" kick, add a tablespoon of cacao nibs to the mixture once it is frozen.

2 large avocados, peeled and pitted

¼ cup unsweetened cocoa powder

2 (13.5-ounce) cans light canned coconut milk

½ cup pure maple sugar or syrup

3 large Medjool dates, pitted

½ teaspoon salt

1 teaspoon pure vanilla extract

Place all the ingredients in a blender and blend until very smooth, stopping and scraping down the sides of the blender container as needed. Process in an ice-cream maker according to the manufacturer's instructions. Alternatively, pour the mixture into a freezer-safe baking dish and cover loosely with plastic wrap. Freeze for 20 minutes, and using an electric hand mixer, blend quickly to mix. Refreeze for 20 minutes, then blend again. Repeat until the mixture is the consistency of gelato. Store in an airtight container for up to 3 weeks, allowing to thaw slightly before serving.

YIELD:

6 SERVINGS

PER SERVING:

232 CALORIES

15.6 G FAT

158 MG SODIUM

337 MG POTASSIUM

23.1 G CARBOHYDRATES

1.8 G PROTEIN

Too Good for You to Be True Chocolate

You'll have a hard time going back to traditional chocolate after tasting this easy concoction, which is sweetened with maple syrup rather than with refined sugar and made with cocoa powder, which is high in protein, iron, and magnesium. It has a deep, dark chocolate flavor and melt-in-your-mouth texture and can be enjoyed as is or used in recipes just like semisweet chocolate. You'll need food-grade cacao butter for this recipe, which can be sourced online or in many natural food and specialty stores. You can use any type of candy mold for these chocolates, but I prefer the silicone or clear plastic types. Silicone ice cube or mini muffin tins also work great.

130 g (9½ tablespoons) food-grade cacao butter

⅓ cup pure maple syrup

1 teaspoon pure vanilla extract

½ cup unsweetened cocoa powder

¼ teaspoon salt

Prepare your silicone chocolate molds or silicone mini muffin tins by placing them on a small, flat cookie sheet that will easily fit into your freezer.

Chop the cacao butter into 1-inch cubes and place in the top of a double boiler. Be sure the pan is totally clean and dry or the chocolate may ruin easily. Heat the double boiler over medium-low heat and keep a watchful eye on the cacao butter as it melts, stirring often to help ensure even melting. When the cacao butter is mostly melted, drizzle in the maple syrup and vanilla extract. Remove from the heat and quickly whisk in the cocoa powder and salt. Pour into your choice of molds and place in the freezer to set for 15 minutes, or until firm. Store in a cool, dry place for up to 1 month.

YIELD:

20 SERVINGS

PER SERVING:

47 CALORIES

3.5 G FAT

32 MG SODIUM

56 MG POTASSIUM

4.7 G CARBOHYDRATES

0.4 G PROTEIN

Chocolate Hazelnut Bites

Chocolate and hazelnut star in these no-bake cookies, which are like little Nutella bites! Hazelnuts and filberts, which are essentially the same nut (*filbert* is the term used in Oregon, the producer of about 98 percent of the hazelnuts grown in the United States), can be used interchangeably in this recipe. These nuts are high in omega-3 and -6 fatty acids as well as manganese.

1 cup raw almonds

1 cup raw hazelnuts or filberts

1 teaspoon pure vanilla extract

½ teaspoon salt

3 tablespoons unsweetened cocoa powder

9 to 10 Medjool dates, pitted

Place the almonds, hazelnuts, vanilla extract, salt, and cocoa powder in a food processor and process until the mixture becomes the texture of coarse cornmeal. Allowing the food processor to run, add one date at a time until the mixture clumps together easily. Try to err on the low side: after eight or nine dates, pinch a section of the mixture together until it sticks to see whether you need another date to bring it all together.

Roll the mixture tightly into 1-inch balls. Store in an airtight container for up to 2 weeks.

YIELD:

20 SERVINGS

PER SERVING:

82 CALORIES

4.8 G FAT

58 MG SODIUM

81 MG POTASSIUM

9.6 G CARBOHYDRATES

2.1 G PROTEIN

White Chocolate Peanut Butter Fudge Bites

Totally peanut buttery and pretty addictive, these fudgy bites taste similar to the peanut butter fudge my mother used to make when I was a kid—except this fudge has no refined sugar or condensed milk for sweetening; instead, maple sugar is used. The key to these is to make sure that all the ingredients are well mixed before pouring into the molds, to ensure silky-smooth fudge that will keep you going back for more.

200 g (about 1⅔ cups) food-grade cacao butter, chopped

1 cup smooth peanut butter

1 teaspoon pure vanilla extract

⅔ cup maple sugar or pure maple or agave syrup

¼ teaspoon salt

Prepare your silicone chocolate molds or silicone mini muffin tins by placing them on a small, flat cookie sheet that will easily fit into your freezer.

In the top of a double boiler, melt the cacao butter over medium-low heat until completely liquefied. Once melted, gradually stir in the peanut butter, vanilla extract, maple sugar, and salt and stir, using a whisk, until totally blended and liquid. Pour into your choice of molds. Place on a flat surface in the freezer and freeze until solid, about 30 minutes. Store in a covered container in the refrigerator for up to 2 weeks.

YIELD:

30 SERVINGS

PER SERVING:

91 CALORIES

7.7 G FAT

59 MG SODIUM

65 MG POTASSIUM

4.6 G CARBOHYDRATES

2.1 G PROTEIN

No need to purchase expensive nondairy milk; simply make your own. Cashew milk is one of my favorite nut milks to make at home because the store-bought kinds can be quite pricey, and unlike almond milk, it requires no straining—just blend and go!

1½ cups raw cashews, soaked in water for 3 hours and drained

4 cups water, plus more to thin as needed

⅛ teaspoon salt

Place the soaked cashews in a blender along with the water and salt and blend until very smooth. If the milk seems too thick for your liking, add up to 1 cup of additional water and blend.

Store in an airtight container for up to 1 week. The milk will separate as it settles, but gently shaking before enjoying will fix it.

YIELD:

6 CUPS

PER ½ CUP SERVING UNSWEETENED:

105 CALORIES

7 G FAT

28 MG SODIUM

98 MG POTASSIUM

7.3 G CARBOHYDRATES

2.7 G PROTEIN

For a sweetened milk, add one or two pitted Medjool dates plus ½ teaspoon of pure vanilla extract. (Per ½ cup sweetened: 115 calories; 7.9 g fat; 28 mg sodium; 98 mg potassium; 8.7 g carbohydrates; 2.8 g protein)

Almond Milk

This versatile nondairy milk works great in so many recipes. It's slightly less creamy than cashew milk and has a milder, almost sweet flavor that works in both sweet and savory applications.

2 cups raw almonds

6 cups water

Pinch of salt

Place the almonds, water, and salt in a blender (a high-speed blender works very well here) and blend until well blended, 6 or 7 minutes. Strain the milk through cheesecloth into a resealable container. Store in the refrigerator for up to 5 days.

YIELD:

12 SERVINGS

PER SERVING:

40 CALORIES

3 G FAT

180 MG SODIUM

0 G POTASSIUM

2 G CARBOHYDRATES

1 G PROTEIN

Simple Cashew Cream   OF

This cashew cream is a fab replacement for whipped cream or sour cream and can be used in a variety of recipes. It makes a delicious appearance in my Caramel Apple Parfaits (page 96).

1½ cups raw cashews, soaked in water for 1 hour and drained

⅓ cup light canned coconut milk

2 teaspoons pure maple syrup, or a dash of stevia

1 teaspoon freshly squeezed lemon juice

Blend the soaked cashews along with the rest of the ingredients in a blender until extra smooth, about 5 minutes, stopping and scraping down the sides of the container as needed. Transfer to a resealable container in the refrigerator and chill until ready to use.

YIELD:

8 SERVINGS

PER SERVING:

158 CALORIES

12.4 G FAT

7 MG SODIUM

150 MG POTASSIUM

10 G CARBOHYDRATES

4.1 G PROTEIN

Creary Cashew Cheese

This cheese makes a lovely appetizer at a party when rolled in chopped pecans and minced fresh parsley, or use it to spread on sandwiches or as a vegetable dip or pâté. Be sure you make the recipe a day ahead of when you plan to serve it, so the flavor has plenty of time to develop. The key to this cheese is the bit of probiotic powder used to give it that tangy, cheesy flavor. Seek out probiotic powder at many health food stores and pharmacies. Feel free to use capsules of the powder (simply open the capsules and pour out the powder) if you cannot locate free-flowing powder.

2 cups raw cashews, soaked in water for 4 hours and drained

1 cup water

1 teaspoon salt

1 tablespoon freshly squeezed lemon juice

1 teaspoon lemon zest

2 teaspoons probiotic powder

¼ cup nutritional yeast flakes

½ teaspoon garlic powder

Place all the ingredients in a food processor and blend until smooth, about 7 minutes, stopping and scraping down the sides of the bowl as needed. Line a large bowl with cheesecloth and place the mixture in a mound on top of the cheesecloth. Twist and secure with a rubber band or by tying with kitchen twine, so that the mixture is taut within the cheesecloth. Place in a colander on top of a baking sheet (to catch any liquid) and let rest for 2 hours. Transfer to the refrigerator and chill overnight.

Store in an airtight container for up to 2 weeks.

YIELD:

12 SERVINGS

PER SERVING:

144 CALORIES

10.8 G FAT

200 MG SODIUM

213 MG POTASSIUM

9.1 G CARBOHYDRATES

5.1 G PROTEIN

Brazil Nut Ricotta

Use this ricotta replica in any recipe you please. It makes a marvelous addition to salads and creamy dips, and as a base for the Ricotta-Stuffed Creminis (page 184). The fat in Brazil nuts is mostly monounsaturated, which is known to lower "bad" (LDL) cholesterol and increase "good" (HDL) cholesterol levels in the blood. They are also one of the highest sources of selenium, which is helpful in preventing coronary artery disease.

2 cups raw Brazil nuts, soaked in water for 2 to 4 hours and drained

⅔ cup water

3 tablespoons freshly squeezed lime juice

½ teaspoon lemon zest

1 teaspoon salt

Place the drained Brazil nuts in a high-speed blender or food processor. Add ⅓ cup of the water and the lime juice, lemon zest, and salt and blend until pureed. Add the remaining ⅓ cup of water and continue to blend until fairly smooth but still a touch grainy, to mimic the texture of ricotta cheese. Store in an airtight container for up to 1 week.

YIELD:

10 SERVINGS

PER SERVING:

49 CALORIES

4.7 G FAT

234 MG SODIUM

62 MG POTASSIUM

2 G CARBOHYDRATES

1.2 G PROTEIN

Parmesan Sprinkles

This little gem of a recipe couldn't be any simpler. Made with almonds, lemon zest, and nutritional yeast, this powerhouse flavor enhancer is a much-loved addition to the pantry. Keep a jar on hand for an easy flavoring for popcorn, or a lovely garnish for a pasta dish—you can sprinkle it on virtually everything from salads to soups to roasted potatoes.

Zest of 1 large lemon (about 1 tablespoon)

1 cup almond meal

⅓ cup nutritional yeast

1½ teaspoons salt

1 teaspoon onion powder

Place all the ingredients in a jar that has a lid. Shake vigorously for 15 seconds. Stir and shake again. Store in an airtight container in the refrigerator for up to 2 months.

YIELD:

20 SERVINGS (10 G EACH SERVING)

PER SERVING:

38 CALORIES

2.5 G FAT

176 MG SODIUM

101 MG POTASSIUM

2.4 G CARBOHYDRATES

1.3 G FIBER

2.2 G PROTEIN

Stealthy Healthy Mayo

This spread doesn't taste exactly like mayo—as it's completely oil free, and mayonnaise (regular and egg free) is basically oil emulsified with a stabilizer—but it does make an incredible replacement if you're looking for a healthier alternative to the traditional stuff. Use it in recipes and spread on sandwiches just as you would regular mayo.

1 cup raw cashews, soaked in water for 2 hours and drained

12.3 ounces light extra-firm silken tofu, drained

2 tablespoons freshly squeezed lemon juice

¼ teaspoon lemon zest

2 tablespoons water

¼ teaspoon garlic powder, or ½ garlic clove

½ teaspoon salt

1 teaspoon cider vinegar

½ teaspoon mustard powder

Mix all the ingredients in a blender until very smooth, making sure to stop and scrape the sides of the blender container periodically. Store in an airtight glass container for up to 10 days in the refrigerator.

YIELD:

20 SERVINGS

PER SERVING:

49 CALORIES

3.5 G FAT

71 MG SODIUM

41 MG POTASSIUM

2.7 G CARBOHYDRATES

2.3 G PROTEIN

CHAPTER 5
LEGUMES

Legumes are the group of vegetables that contain beans, peas, and lentils, each boasting exceptional nutritional properties. Legumes contain a high amount of fiber and typically a low amount of fat as well as a good bit of protein. They are easy to add to all sorts of recipes and offer great flavor and nutrition. From flavorful Crispy Baked Falafel (page 142) and hummus (pages 157 and 158) to Peanut Butter Black Bean Brownie Bites (page 159), these recipes celebrate the versatility of legumes, and how they can go far beyond just baked beans.

Note: Many beans are available dried or canned. I prefer to cook my own beans (with less than ¼ teaspoon of salt per pound of beans) for best flavor and texture, but I totally understand the convenience of using canned beans, so I'll leave it up to you in these recipes. The nutritional info given for recipes featuring beans is for cooked and lightly salted beans, so keep in mind the sodium counts will increase if you use salted canned beans.

Crispy Baked Falafel

Falafel has long been a favorite main course of mine, as chickpea-based falafel patties are generally gluten-free by default. Still, I've never loved the fact that they are usually fried. These have all the charm of traditional falafel with a fraction of the fat, thanks to baking instead of frying. Serve the falafel over a bed of mixed veggies or greens and top with hummus or your favorite salad dressing (try the White Bean Ranch Dressing on page 161) for a deliciously filling meal.

4 cloves garlic

1 large shallot or small onion

2 cups cooked chickpeas, drained and rinsed

1 cup chickpea flour

1 teaspoon ground cumin

¾ teaspoon salt

1 teaspoon baking powder

¼ cup finely chopped fresh cilantro

¼ cup finely chopped fresh parsley

1 teaspoon olive oil

Preheat your oven to 400°F and place the unpeeled garlic and shallot in a small shallow baking dish. Roast, uncovered, for 25 to 30 minutes, until fragrant and very tender. Let cool for a few minutes, until they're safe to touch. Carefully peel the garlic and shallot and place in the bowl of a food processor.

Add the chickpeas to the roasted garlic and shallot and blend until smooth, stopping and scraping down the sides of the bowl as needed.

Transfer the pureed chickpeas to a large bowl and use a large spoon to stir in the chickpea flour, cumin, salt, and baking powder until very well combined. Fold in the cilantro and parsley. Use clean hands to work the mixture into a dough. If it's slightly sticky, add a touch more chickpea flour.

YIELD:

12 SERVINGS

PER SERVING:

190 CALORIES

3.5 G FAT

161 MG SODIUM

503 MG POTASSIUM

31.5 G CARBOHYDRATES

9.8 G PROTEIN

Pinch into twelve equal-size balls and shape into pucks about 1½ inches x ½ inch. Brush each side very lightly with the olive oil and place on a parchment paper– or silicone mat–covered cookie sheet. Bake for 15 minutes, flip, and bake for an additional 15 to 17 minutes, until golden and crispy on both sides and cooked throughout. Enjoy hot.

An excellent gadget to have around the house if you love tofu, but don't love how long it takes to press, is a TofuXpress. These guys run about $30, but they are worth the money just in the paper towels you save, not to mention they are much faster (about 30 minutes to press a block) than the traditional method of pressing, which can sometimes take hours.

Popcorn Tofu

Much like popcorn chicken, these scrumptious tofu bites are crispy and tender, and they also happen to be irresistible. Give yourself a little extra time to make this recipe, as you'll need about one day to freeze and thaw the tofu. Freezing transforms the tofu's texture into a denser, meatier version of itself that works wonderfully in this simple recipe. These go great with the Beyond Good BBQ Sauce (page 101).

1 (14-ounce) package extra-firm tofu, well drained and pressed

½ cup chickpea flour

½ cup water

1 teaspoon salt

½ teaspoon garlic powder

½ teaspoon freshly ground black pepper

1 cup almond meal

Place the drained, pressed tofu into a freezer-safe resealable plastic bag and freeze for at least 6 hours. Remove from the freezer and allow to thaw, again squeezing any excess water from the tofu. Slice the tofu evenly into bite-size squares.

Preheat your oven to 400°F and cover a large baking sheet with parchment paper.

In a small bowl, whisk together the chickpea flour, water, salt, garlic powder, and black pepper.

Place the almond meal in a separate bowl.

Gently dip each square of tofu first into the chickpea flour mixture—allowing any excess to drip off the tofu—and then into the almond meal to coat evenly. Place directly on the parchment paper and repeat until all the tofu is coated. Bake for 15 minutes, flip, and bake for an additional 20 minutes, until the tofu is evenly browned on all sides.

Serve hot.

YIELD:

6 SERVINGS

PER SERVING:

227 CALORIES

15.9 G FAT

206 MG SODIUM

374 MG POTASSIUM

11.7 G CARBOHYDRATES

13.5 G PROTEIN

Avocado Chick'n Salad

Just like deli-style chicken salad, except chickpeas stand in for the chicken and avocado replaces the mayo. This recipe makes a delicious meal when served atop a bed of greens, or as a filling in a collard wrap. Avocados are high in both fiber and omega-6 fatty acids. To retain the most nutrients—which lie in highest concentration closest to the peel and pit—opt for peeling an avocado similarly to a banana, by slicing a few shallow cuts to start, and removing the skin completely by peeling it back with your fingertips.

¾ cup grapes, quartered

2 scallions, chopped

2 stalks celery, sliced

2 cups cooked chickpeas, drained and rinsed

1 teaspoon salt

1 large avocado

Juice and zest of ½ lemon

¼ teaspoon freshly ground black pepper

½ tablespoon white balsamic vinegar

Place the grapes, scallions, and celery in a large bowl. Place the chickpeas on top and sprinkle with ½ teaspoon of the salt. Mash the chickpeas for about 20 seconds, using a potato masher or large fork (not all will be mashed, and some of the grapes will get smashed; that's okay—you want some chunks to get that chicken salad texture).

In a medium-size bowl, place the avocado flesh along with the lemon juice and zest, the remaining ½ teaspoon of salt, black pepper and balsamic vinegar. Mash with a fork and then stir until smooth. Mix with the chickpea mixture until well coated.

Serve immediately or chill before serving. Keeps in an airtight container for up to 1 day.

YIELD:

8 SERVINGS

PER SERVING:

241 CALORIES

8.0 G FAT

308 MG SODIUM

827 MG POTASSIUM

34.5 G CARBOHYDRATES

10.8 G PROTEIN

Rainbow Veggie Chili

Colorful and flavorful, this chili recipe makes a good amount and freezes well, so if you can't finish a whole batch, simply put the leftovers in an airtight freezer-safe container and thaw by warming gently over medium heat.

½ small red onion, diced

1 cup quartered white button mushrooms

1 medium-size red potato, skin on, diced

½ small yellow zucchini, diced

½ orange bell pepper, seeded and diced

½ red bell pepper, seeded and diced

½ yellow bell pepper, seeded and diced

2 cloves garlic, minced

2 cups chopped collard greens

5 cups vegan vegetable broth, such as Super Easy Veggie Broth (page 171)

1 teaspoon salt

½ teaspoon ground coriander

3 teaspoons ground chili seasoning

½ teaspoon ground allspice

1 teaspoon ground turmeric

1 teaspoon paprika

½ cup fresh, frozen, or canned corn

1 cup cooked black beans, drained and rinsed

1 cup cooked kidney beans, drained and rinsed

1 cup cooked great northern beans, drained and rinsed

2½ tablespoons chickpea flour mixed with 3 tablespoons water until very smooth

½ avocado, diced

2 to 4 lime wedges

¼ cup chopped fresh cilantro

In a large stockpot, combine the onion, mushrooms, potato, zucchini, peppers, garlic, collard greens, vegetable broth, salt, and spices and bring to a boil. Lower the heat to medium-low to retain a constant simmer. Cook for 10 minutes, or until the potatoes begin to soften, then add the corn, black beans, and kidney beans.

In a food processor, puree the great northern beans and then blend into the rest of the ingredients in the stockpot. Drizzle in the chickpea flour slurry and simmer over medium heat for about 10 minutes, or until thickened. Do not undercook or the raw chickpea flour flavor will come through, which isn't at all desirable.

Serve with the avocado, a squeeze of lime, and fresh cilantro.

YIELD:

10 SERVINGS

PER SERVING:

211 CALORIES

3.6 G FAT

601 MG SODIUM

913 MG POTASSIUM

34.4 G CARBOHYDRATES

13.0 G PROTEIN

Zesty Black Bean Soup

I've had plenty of black bean soups in my day and I've often been underwhelmed, but not with this recipe! The allspice and ginger plus a touch of sweetness from the coconut palm sugar give it a bit of unexpected zing.

1 cup seeded and chopped red bell pepper

1 teaspoon grated fresh ginger

1 red onion or 3 shallots, diced

1 cup sliced mushrooms

1 jalapeño or serrano pepper, seeded and diced

1 clove garlic, minced

1 teaspoon ground allspice

2 teaspoons fresh thyme

2 tablespoons water

1¼ teaspoons salt

2 tablespoons coconut palm or maple sugar

5 cups salted vegan vegetable broth, such as Super Easy Veggie Broth (page 171)

3½ cups cooked black beans, drained and rinsed

¼ cup minced fresh chives

In a medium-size saucepan or stockpot, combine the bell pepper, grated ginger, onion, mushrooms, jalapeño, garlic, allspice, thyme, and water. Sprinkle lightly with ¾ teaspoon of the salt. Sauté over medium heat until the vegetables are tender, about 7 minutes. Add the remaining ½ teaspoon of salt and the coconut palm sugar, vegetable broth, and black beans and simmer for 15 to 20 minutes, until fragrant and long enough for the flavors to meld. Serve hot, topped with chives.

YIELD:

8 SERVINGS

PER SERVING:

251 CALORIES

1.7 G FAT

534 MG SODIUM

1071 MG POTASSIUM

44.3 G CARBOHYDRATES

15.9 G PROTEIN

Roasted Corn and Cilantro Chili

This recipe relies on the sweetness of corn to balance out the spices throughout and refried beans to thicken the chili. Navy beans add a creamy white contrast to this colorful dish and are high in protein, fiber, and iron. If you don't have fresh corn on the cob, thaw about 1½ cups of frozen corn and sauté lightly over medium heat until browned for a similar effect.

2 ears corn, shucked

¼ teaspoon olive oil

½ onion, diced
   (about ¾ cup)

1 bell pepper, any color,
   seeded and diced

2 cloves garlic, minced

½ teaspoon salt, plus
   more if desired

2 tablespoons water

2 teaspoons ground chili
   seasoning, plus more
   if desired

1 (28-ounce) can diced
   tomatoes

1 (16-ounce) can fat-
   free refried beans

1 (16-ounce) can navy
   beans, or 2 cups
   cooked, drained
   and rinsed

1 cup chopped fresh
   cilantro

Preheat your oven to 400°F. Lightly rub the corn with the olive oil and wrap loosely in aluminum foil. Place on a baking sheet and bake for 60 minutes, until fragrant. Let cool slightly before cutting the kernels off the cob.

In a stockpot, combine the onion, bell pepper, garlic, salt, water, and chili seasoning and heat over medium-high heat for about 7 minutes, stirring often, until the onion is translucent and the pepper is tender. Stir in the diced tomatoes, refried beans, navy beans, roasted corn kernels, and up to ¾ teaspoon of additional salt and up to 4 more teaspoons of chili seasoning, if desired. The refried beans will need to warm a bit before they blend in easily. Heat for about 10 minutes, over medium-low heat, stirring often. Stir in the chopped cilantro and serve hot.

YIELD:

8 SERVINGS

PER SERVING:

280 CALORIES

1.5 G FAT

691 MG SODIUM

1162 MG
POTASSIUM

51.9 G
CARBOHYDRATES

17.1 G PROTEIN

Sunshine Breakfast UnScramble

This easy recipe is called an "unscramble" because no sautéing is needed to bring together this breakfast dish, which boasts a savory, satisfying base and flavorful roasted veggies. Simply mix, bake, and toss together! The inclusion of black salt—which is actually not black, but light pink or purple—adds an authentic "eggy" taste to the dish.

½ cup chickpea flour

½ cup water

¾ teaspoon salt

½ teaspoon black salt

2 cloves garlic, minced

½ teaspoon ground cumin

1 tablespoon olive oil

1 (14-ounce) block extra-firm tofu, drained and pressed

1 cup chopped broccoli florets

6 cherry tomatoes, halved

Preheat your oven to 375°F and line a 9 x 13-inch cake pan with parchment paper. In a large bowl, whisk together the chickpea flour, water, ½ teaspoon of the salt, and the black salt, garlic, cumin, and ½ tablespoon of the olive oil until very well mixed. Crumble in the tofu and mix gently, but thoroughly. Spread in an even layer on two thirds of the prepared cake pan, so that the mixture is about 1 inch thick. Arrange the broccoli and tomatoes on the other third of the pan, drizzle lightly with the remaining ½ tablespoon of olive oil, and sprinkle with the remaining ¼ teaspoon of salt. Bake for 25 minutes, or until golden brown. Gently toss the veggies and the scramble together and serve hot.

YIELD:

4 SERVINGS

PER SERVING:

283 CALORIES

10.3 G FAT

787 MG SODIUM

926 MG POTASSIUM

28.9 G CARBOHYDRATES

24.3 G PROTEIN

Red Bean Sweet Potato Salad

Red beans are packed with iron, protein, and even a little bit of calcium. Use kidney or another type of red bean in this recipe, for a lovely salad that tastes great chilled or served slightly warm.

2 average-size sweet potatoes, peeled and cut into ½-inch cubes

1 teaspoon olive oil

¼ teaspoon salt, plus more to taste

1¼ cups cooked red beans, drained and rinsed

1 cup fresh or frozen corn (thaw if frozen)

3 scallions, chopped

¼ cup finely chopped fresh parsley

¼ teaspoon freshly ground black pepper

2 tablespoons freshly squeezed lime juice

1 teaspoon pure maple syrup (optional)

2 tablespoons Stealthy Healthy Mayo (page 139) or other vegan mayo

½ teaspoon ground coriander

Preheat your oven to 425°F and line a large baking sheet with parchment paper or a silicone mat. In a medium-size bowl, toss the sweet potatoes with the olive oil and spread in a single layer on the prepared baking sheet. Sprinkle with the salt. Bake for 15 to 20 minutes, until the potatoes are tender and golden on edges. Remove from the heat and allow to cool for 15 minutes. Transfer to a medium-size bowl along with the red beans, corn, scallions, and parsley. In a small bowl, whisk together the remaining ingredients and toss with the potato mixture. Salt lightly and stir. Serve at room temperature or slightly warmed.

YIELD:

6 SERVINGS

PER SERVING:

267 CALORIES

2.7 G FAT

148 MG SODIUM

1248 MG POTASSIUM

52.4 G CARBOHYDRATES

10.7 G PROTEIN

Orange Lentil Salad

This light and citrusy salad is a great way to enjoy lentils if you're not normally a fan. Some find lentils to be a little too "earthy" in flavor, but their flavor can be mellowed when lightly sweetened and tossed with fresh herbs. To supreme— or segment—an orange, cut off the top and bottom and then carve away enough of the peel to expose the orange flesh, by using a paring knife, curving the cuts out and downward to follow the spherical shape of the orange. Once the peel is removed, simply slice out each of the wedges to free the segments from the membrane.

2 cups cooked green lentils, drained and rinsed

½ teaspoon ground coriander

½ teaspoon ground cumin

1 teaspoon salt

1 cup cherry tomatoes, halved or quartered if large

1 carrot, shredded

1 orange, supremed and cut into small pieces

½ teaspoon orange zest

½ cup chopped fresh parsley

2 tablespoons chopped fresh mint

Place the lentils in a large bowl and toss with the coriander, cumin, and salt to evenly combine. Stir in the remaining ingredients and let rest for 1 hour in the refrigerator before serving.

YIELD:

6 SERVINGS

PER SERVING:

253 CALORIES

0.9 G FAT

404 MG SODIUM

811 MG POTASSIUM

44.8 G CARBOHYDRATES

17.4 G PROTEIN

Tempeh and Snow Peas

This easy "peasy" meal can be prepped in less than 5 minutes, and after that you have a good bit of downtime before cooking while the tempeh marinates. Feel free to marinate this for even longer than the suggested time, up to 6 hours. The longer the marinade, the better the flavor.

1 (8-ounce) block tempeh, cut into bite-size cubes

2 tablespoons gluten-free soy sauce, plus more for serving

1 tablespoon freshly squeezed lime juice

1 clove garlic, grated

¼ cup pineapple juice

½ teaspoon grated fresh ginger

1 cup snow peas

Place the cubed tempeh in a small shallow dish that can accommodate each cube so that they are in a single layer. In a small bowl, whisk together the 2 tablespoons of soy sauce and the lime juice, garlic, pineapple juice, and grated ginger. Pour onto the tempeh and let marinate at least 1 hour.

Transfer the tempeh and the remaining marinade liquid to a large skillet. Add the snow peas and sauté over medium-high heat, stirring occasionally to prevent sticking or burning, until the tempeh is browned on all sides and the snow peas are tender, about 10 minutes. Sprinkle with up to ½ teaspoon more soy sauce, or to taste.

Serve hot.

YIELD:

4 SERVINGS

PER SERVING:

195 CALORIES

9.1 G FAT

498 MG SODIUM

496 MG POTASSIUM

14.6 G CARBOHYDRATES

17.4 G PROTEIN

Pesto Haricots Verts

Pesto helps transfer these green beans into something wonderful. *Haricot vert* is French for "green bean," and I love them as they tend to be smaller, thinner, and more tender than traditional string beans. Seek them out at farmers' markets in the spring.

1 pound haricots verts

½ teaspoon salt

¼ teaspoon freshly ground black pepper

½ cup Walnut Arugula Pesto (page 43)

Preheat your oven to 400°F and line a large baking sheet with parchment paper. Arrange the beans so that they lay in an even single layer on the sheet. Evenly sprinkle with the salt and pepper and roast for 12 to 15 minutes, until crisp and tender.

Place the beans in a large bowl and toss with the pesto to coat. Serve immediately.

YIELD:

6 SERVINGS

PER SERVING:

111 CALORIES

8.7 G FAT

329 MG SODIUM

1 MG POTASSIUM

4.7 G CARBOHYDRATES

2.8 G PROTEIN

Oil-Free Hummus

This recipe is for those who love hummus, but not the added fat of oil and tahini. Instead, chia seeds are used to add creaminess to this dip. The sliced garlic clove adds a nice zing, but is totally optional if you'd prefer a milder flavor. Serve this hummus well chilled, with fresh cut veggies or even fresh cut fruit. I adore this hummus served with crisp apple slices.

3 cups cooked or canned chickpeas, peeled (not needed if using canned), drained, and rinsed

1 teaspoon lemon zest

2 tablespoons freshly squeezed lemon juice

1 clove garlic, sliced (optional)

½ teaspoon salt

⅓ cup water

Pinch of ground cumin

1 teaspoon ground chia seeds

1 tablespoon almond meal (use tahini or sunflower butter for nut allergy)

Place the chickpeas; lemon zest and juice; garlic, if using; salt; and water in a food processor and blend until very smooth, stopping and scraping down the sides of the bowl often, about 5 minutes. Add the cumin, chia seeds, and almond meal and blend for an additional 2 minutes, or until fluffy. Chill and serve cold. Store the hummus in an airtight container in the refrigerator for up to 1 week.

YIELD:

15 SERVINGS

PER SERVING:

149 CALORIES

2.6 G FAT

88 MG SODIUM

357 MG POTASSIUM

24.5 G CARBOHYDRATES

7.8 G PROTEIN

Pizza Hummus

Two of my favorite comfort foods come together in one delightfully light dip. Be sure to use the best-quality oil-free sun-dried tomatoes you can get your hands on, for best results. "Pizza spice" is a combination of dried herbs (oregano, fennel seeds, rosemary, and basil) mixed with a little dried garlic and onion. If you can't find it, feel free to season as you please. I personally adore the premixed spice blends, because they really nail that authentic pizza parlor flavor.

3 cups cooked or canned chickpeas, peeled (not needed if using canned), drained and rinsed

⅓ cup oil-free sun-dried tomatoes, soaked in water for 30 minutes and drained

1 tablespoon olive oil

½ cup plus 2 tablespoons cold water

2 teaspoons pizza spice

1 clove garlic

½ teaspoon salt

1 tablespoon freshly squeezed lemon juice

Place all the ingredients in a food processor and blend for 6 to 7 minutes, stopping to scrape down the sides of the bowl often. Serve with (gluten-free) toasts, crackers, tortilla chips, or as a spread on a sandwich or in a wrap. It's all good!

YIELD:

15 SERVINGS

PER SERVING:

157 CALORIES

3.4 G FAT

110 MG SODIUM

393 MG POTASSIUM

25.0 G CARBOHYDRATES

7.9 G PROTEIN

Made with black beans and without oil, these brownies take the cake for being a healthy dessert that's chock-full of protein. Sweeten with unrefined cane sugar, coconut palm sugar, or even maple sugar.

2 tablespoons flaxseed meal

3 tablespoons water

1²/₃ cups cooked black beans, drained and rinsed

¼ cup smooth peanut butter

¾ cup unsweetened cocoa powder

½ teaspoon salt

1½ teaspoons pure vanilla extract

²/₃ cup unrefined sugar, such as coconut palm or maple sugar

1½ teaspoons baking powder

¼ cup crushed walnuts (optional)

Preheat your oven to 350°F. In a small bowl, mix together the flaxseed meal and the water and allow to rest for 5 minutes, or until gelled. In the bowl of a food processor, combine the black beans, peanut butter, cocoa powder, salt, vanilla extract, unrefined sugar, baking powder, and prepared flaxseed gel, and blend until smooth, stopping and scraping down the sides of the bowl as needed. Drop evenly among sixteen mini muffin cups and sprinkle the tops with the crushed walnuts, if using. Bake for 30 minutes. Let cool briefly and then use a knife to gently loosen the brownies to remove. Store for up to 1 week in an airtight container.

YIELD:

16 SERVINGS

PER SERVING:

152 CALORIES

4.3 G FAT

83 MG SODIUM

492 MG POTASSIUM

24.3 G CARBOHYDRATES

6.7 G PROTEIN

Lighten Up Pizza Crust

This pizza crust couldn't get any easier to prepare and it's lighter than your average crust—plus, it boasts a good amount of protein, thanks to the chickpea flour. Bake this as directed before adding toppings. When you're ready to top the crust, add your favorite toppings and then bake again at 450°F for 10 to 15 minutes.

1½ cups chickpea flour

½ cup superfine brown rice flour

1 teaspoon salt

1 teaspoon baking powder

4 tablespoons olive oil

1¼ cups water

Preheat your oven to 375°F. Prepare a large baking sheet by covering with two sheets of parchment paper (stacked) or a large silicone mat.

In a large bowl, whisk together the chickpea flour, brown rice flour, salt, baking powder, olive oil, and water and mix until super smooth, about fifty strokes. Spread in an even layer, about ½ inch thick, on the prepared baking surface. Shape into a circle or rectangle, using a flat silicone spatula or the back of a wooden spoon.

Bake for 23 minutes, or until baked through and the bottom of the crust easily separates from the top layer of paper.

YIELD:

8 SERVINGS

PER SERVING:

200 CALORIES

8.6 G FAT

302 MG SODIUM

392 MG POTASSIUM

25 G CARBOHYDRATES

7.4 G PROTEIN

White Bean Ranch Dressing

This easy salad topper tastes a lot like traditional ranch dressing, yet is totally free of dairy. Instead, white beans are used along with silken tofu to create a creamy, flavorful dressing.

12.4 ounces extra-firm silken tofu, drained

¾ cup cooked white beans, drained and rinsed

2 teaspoons garlic powder

2 teaspoons freshly squeezed lemon juice

2 tablespoons dill pickle juice

1½ teaspoons salt

3 heaping tablespoons very finely chopped fresh chives

2 tablespoons very finely chopped fresh dill

1 tablespoon finely chopped fresh parsley

In a blender, combine the tofu, white beans, garlic powder, lemon juice, pickle juice, and salt and blend until very smooth. Transfer to a medium-size bowl and fold in the chives, dill, and parsley. Stir well and cover. Let rest in the refrigerator for 1 hour before serving. Store in an airtight container for up to 4 days.

YIELD:

10 SERVINGS

PER SERVING:

74 CALORIES

0.8 G FAT

694 MG SODIUM

375 MG POTASSIUM

10.7 G CARBOHYDRATES

6.3 G PROTEIN

CHAPTER 6

SQUASH, ROOTS, & MUSHROOMS

These underrated veggies are the stars of many great recipes, but some people don't feel comfortable going beyond such basics as potatoes and carrots. Enhance your everyday meals by adding some new-to-you starchy squashes, rugged root vegetables, and meaty mushrooms, which are all great foods to add bulk to your diet without a lot of added fat. Never had a rutabaga? The Carrot Rutabaga Butternut Bisque (page 179) is a lovely intro recipe. Dive into a Delicata Squash Millet Bowl (page 183) and relish the simple red radish in my recipe for Cucumber, Mango, and Radish Salad (page 187).

Yukon-Stuffed Poblanos

This dish is spicy! The piquancy (spiciness) of poblano peppers can vary, depending on a variety of factors, from age and to genetics to location grown and environmental stressors (such as temperature). To be sure I'm not serving inedibly hot peppers to friends and family, I like to taste a small section of the pepper before stuffing, to make sure they offer a pleasant level of heat. For those who'd rather play it mild, replace the poblanos with medium-size bell peppers of any color.

3 medium-size Yukon gold potatoes, skin on

¾ teaspoon salt

3 tablespoons Parmesan Sprinkles (page 138)

¼ cup chopped fresh parsley

3 poblano peppers

Preheat your oven to 400°F. Place the potatoes on a baking sheet and pierce several holes in each, using a fork. Bake for 45 minutes, or until the skin is dark golden and the potatoes are tender. Let cool for 15 minutes.

Place the whole baked potatoes in a food processor along with the salt, Parmesan Sprinkles, and parsley. Process until the mixture is smooth, about 1 minute.

Scrub the poblanos and then slice one slit lengthwise to open; carefully remove the seeds and the membrane completely. Gently pry open the peppers and stuff with the potato mixture. Close the peppers. Place on a baking sheet and cover loosely with foil. Bake for 40 to 45 minutes, or until the peppers are tender. Serve hot with Superfresh Salsa (page 83).

YIELD:

3 SERVINGS

PER SERVING:

183 CALORIES

3.3 G FAT

605 MG SODIUM

949 MG POTASSIUM

36.2 G CARBOHYDRATES

5.8 G PROTEIN

Zucchini-Laced Fusilli

This pasta dish is a good lower-calorie choice because half of the bulk of the recipe is made from zucchini, making it much lighter than eating a bowlful of pasta. Increase the zucchini content and it becomes even lighter! It also makes quite a bit, and stores well in the refrigerator, making it a great dish to enjoy for a couple of days if you're looking for an easy lunch or dinner option. To reheat, simply add 2 tablespoons of water to a saucepan and heat gently over medium heat until warmed throughout.

14 ounces brown rice fusilli pasta

Salt

SAUCE

1⅔ cups raw cashews, soaked in water for 3 hours and drained

1 tablespoon rice vinegar

½ teaspoon salt, plus more to taste

½ cup water

SAUTÉ

4 tomatoes, blanched and skins removed, chopped

1 cup packed fresh basil, chopped

2 large shallots, sliced into strips

1 cup raisins

2 cloves garlic, minced

1 teaspoon salt

3 zucchini, sliced into wide ribbons, using a vegetable peeler

Cook the pasta according to the package directions, rinsing with cold water and then tossing with a little salt after cooking.

Make the sauce: In a food processor, blend together the cashews, rice vinegar, ½ teaspoon of salt, and water until very smooth, about 8 minutes, stopping and scraping down the sides of the bowl as necessary. Toss with the pasta to fully coat and stir in up to 1 teaspoon additional salt, to taste.

Make the sauté: In a large, nonstick skillet, toss the tomatoes, basil, shallots, raisins, garlic, and salt together and cook over medium to medium-high heat until the shallots and raisins are soft, about 7 minutes. Add the zucchini ribbons and cook just until wilted. Gently stir the sautéed vegetables into the pasta just enough to mix. Serve immediately.

YIELD:

10 SERVINGS

PER SERVING:

279 CALORIES

9.9 G FAT

246 MG SODIUM

432 MG POTASSIUM

48.6 G CARBOHYDRATES

6.6 G PROTEIN

Magnificent Mushroom Pizza

This pizza looks great topped with a variety of mushrooms. Feel free to choose whatever mushrooms you like; just be sure to slice thinly for even cooking, or make it easy by using a mixed mushroom blend, which you can usually find in the produce sections of most grocery stores. Instead of sauce, the pizza features a smidgen of hummus as the base.

1 recipe Lighten Up Pizza Crust (page 160), baked

⅓ cup plain hummus

2 cups mixed mushrooms, any varieties, thinly sliced

1 teaspoon olive oil

1 tablespoon Parmesan Sprinkles (page 138)

1 tablespoon minced fresh oregano leaves

Pinch of salt

Freshly ground black pepper

Preheat your oven to 450°F. Place the pizza crust on a pizza stone or a large parchment paper–lined baking sheet. Spread the hummus thinly and evenly onto the crust as you would pizza sauce. Arrange the sliced mushrooms evenly on the hummus, and drizzle evenly with the olive oil. Sprinkle with the Parmesan Sprinkles and oregano leaves, and then lightly salt and pepper to taste. Bake for 15 minutes, or until the mushrooms are tender and the crust is crisp and golden brown on the edges. Slice and serve hot.

YIELD:

8 SERVINGS

PER SERVING:

237 CALORIES

11 G FAT

375 MG SODIUM

472 MG POTASSIUM

27.2 G CARBOHYDRATES

9.9 G PROTEIN

Rustic Ratatouille

For superfast prep, use a mandoline or slicing disk for a food processor, which will ensure even slicing for all of the veggies in this dish. This dish is great served alone or on a bed of mashed potatoes, quinoa, forbidden rice, or your favorite grain, and also makes a tasty topping for pasta and the Lighten Up Pizza Crust (page 160).

2 medium-size tomatoes, greens removed

1 head garlic, top trimmed to expose cloves

2 tablespoons olive oil, plus more for drizzling and baking dish

1 Japanese eggplant

1 yellow summer squash, unpeeled

1 green zucchini, unpeeled

1 long red pepper, seeded

1 very large carrot

2 heaping tablespoons tomato paste

½ teaspoon salt

2 tablespoons fresh thyme leaves

1 tablespoon oregano leaves

Fresh ground black pepper

Pinch of smoked salt

Preheat your oven to 400°F. Place the tomatoes and garlic head on a baking sheet. Drizzle with a touch of olive oil. Roast for 45 to 60 minutes. Remove from the oven, let cool, and then remove skins from the tomatoes and the roasted garlic cloves from their head.

Decrease the oven temperature to 375°F. Slice the eggplant, squash, zucchini, red pepper, and carrot into even slices about ⅛ to ¼ of an inch thick.

In a food processor, blend the roasted tomatoes and garlic with the tomato paste, salt, and 2 tablespoons of olive oil until smooth. Spread three quarters of the sauce in the bottom of a lightly oiled ceramic baking dish. Arrange the sliced vegetables in a spiral ring, alternating the colors. Drizzle with olive oil (1½ table-spoons) and the remainder of the sauce. Top with the fresh thyme, oregano, black pepper, and smoked salt.

Cover with parchment paper and bake for 55 minutes.

YIELD:

6 SERVINGS

PER SERVING:

100 CALORIES

5.3 G FAT

277 MG SODIUM

622 MG POTASSIUM

13.4 G CARBOHYDRATES

2.7 G PROTEIN

Super Easy Veggie Broth

I've yet to come across a store-bought veggie broth that even comes close to comparing to homemade, flavor-wise. In case you didn't pick it up from the title, it's also super easy to make. Vegetable broth is a fabulous recipe to prepare ahead (think: big batch on Sundays), as it can easily be frozen and then thawed for later use. Frozen and stored properly, the broth can keep for up to 6 months. Freeze it in small ice cube trays and add a cube or two to soups, stews, and other dishes, to add a burst of flavor whenever needed.

1 onion, peeled and chopped

1 cup chopped carrot

2 cups chopped celery or celeriac

3 collard or kale leaves, stems and all

1 tomato

5 button or cremini mushrooms

1 clove garlic

6 cups water

1 teaspoon salt, or to taste

Place all the ingredients in a large stockpot and bring to a boil over medium heat. Lower the heat to low or medium-low and simmer, uncovered, for 30 minutes. Allow the broth to cool for about 20 minutes, and then strain through cheesecloth or a fine-mesh strainer. Discard the cooked vegetables and allow the broth to cool before storing in an airtight container, or use immediately in a recipe.

YIELD:

6 SERVINGS

PER SERVING:

27 CALORIES

0.2 G FAT

438 MG SODIUM

202 MG POTASSIUM

5.9 G CARBOHYDRATES

1.0 G PROTEIN

Spaghetti Squash with Broccoli and Button Mushrooms

Spaghetti squash has long been a favorite of mine at dinnertime due to its ability to stand in for traditional pasta. Be sure not to overcook the squash in this recipe, lest you end up with mushy "noodles." It's best to shoot on the low side of the cooking time and check the squash by gently running a fork over the flesh. If it separates into strands easily, it's done!

1 medium-size spaghetti squash

½ cup nutritional yeast flakes

½ teaspoon salt

1 teaspoon ground cumin

1 cup chopped broccoli florets

6 button mushrooms, sliced

⅓ cup diced red onion (about ½ small onion)

¼ cup water

¾ teaspoon salt

Preheat your oven to 375°F. Slice the spaghetti squash in half and remove the seeds. Place cut side down on a rimmed metal baking sheet and add 3 tablespoons of water. Bake for 45 to 55 minutes, or until the "spaghetti" strands come away from the squash's skin easily with a fork. Do not overcook, or else your squash will become mushy.

Gently scrape the spaghetti squash from the skin and place in a large bowl. In a small bowl, whisk together the nutritional yeast flakes, salt, and cumin. Toss evenly with the squash, using a large fork.

In a large skillet, place the broccoli florets, mushrooms, red onion, and ¼ cup of water, and then sprinkle evenly with the salt. Heat over medium-high heat, stirring occasionally, until the broccoli is bright green and the mushrooms tender. Plate the spaghetti squash and then top with the sautéed vegetables. Serve hot.

YIELD:

4 SERVINGS

PER SERVING:

114 CALORIES

1.8 G FAT

764 MG SODIUM

743 MG POTASSIUM

17.9 G CARBOHYDRATES

11.4 G PROTEIN

Brilliant Beet Soup

A gorgeous recipe to make a brightly colored pureed soup that is delightful on the eyes—and it happens to taste pretty wonderful as well. If you think you're not a fan of beets, this recipe may just be the one to convert you as the umami flavor of the tomatoes mellows out the earthy beets.

3 medium-size tomatoes, any variety

2 average-size beets or 4 small beets, cleaned and chopped

1 small apple, cored and quartered

2 cloves garlic

Salt

3½ cups salted vegan vegetable broth, such as Super Easy Veggie Broth (page 171)

Preheat your oven to 400°F and place the tomatoes, chopped beets, apple, and garlic cloves in a metal baking dish lined with an oversize square of foil. Salt lightly and fold the pouch over to loosely cover the beets, tomatoes, apple, and garlic. Bake for 45 minutes, or until the beets are tender. Remove the tops from the tomatoes.

Transfer the cooked tomatoes, beets, apple, and garlic to a blender and add 1 cup of the vegetable broth. Puree until smooth and then gradually add the rest of the vegetable broth, to thin. Puree again and then serve immediately, or transfer to a saucepan to warm gently if desired.

YIELD:

4 SERVINGS

PER SERVING:

74 CALORIES

1.5 G FAT

858 MG SODIUM

558 MG POTASSIUM

15.4 G CARBOHYDRATES

6.0 G PROTEIN

Sweet Potato Cauliflower Soup

Since I first shared this recipe on my blog, it has become a huge hit, with millions of views and a lot of fans. Luckily, it's as nutritious as it is delicious and truly couldn't be much easier to whip up. The slightly sweet, yet hearty, flavor and brilliant orange color of the sweet potato pairs beautifully with the robust roasted cauliflower.

1 large head cauliflower (about 7-inch diameter)

A few pinches of garam masala (optional)

½ teaspoon olive oil

Salt

3 medium-size to large sweet potatoes, peeled and cut into 1-inch pieces

1 sweet onion, diced

2 cloves garlic

7 cups water

First, preheat your oven to 400°F and cut your cauliflower into bite-size pieces. Sprinkle the cauliflower lightly with garam masala, if using. Place the cauliflower on an ungreased cookie sheet and lightly drizzle with olive oil. Salt lightly and evenly. Roast until golden brown on top and tender but not mushy, 20 to 30 minutes. There's no need to flip the cauliflower; just remove from oven and let cool while you cook the rest of the soup.

In a large stockpot, bring the sweet potatoes, onion, garlic, and water to a boil. Add ¾ teaspoon of salt and stir. Lower the heat and keep at a constant simmer until the sweet potatoes are tender, 10 to 15 minutes. Add the cooked cauliflower and divide the soup into two equal parts.

Allow the soup to cool slightly and then blend one part of the soup in a blender until very smooth. Combine with second part of the soup and stir. Salt to taste and rewarm over medium heat, if needed.

YIELD:

6 SERVINGS

PER SERVING:

112 CALORIES

0.6 G FAT

320 MG SODIUM

779 MG POTASSIUM

25.3 G CARBOHYDRATES

2.3 G PROTEIN

Cream of Shiitake Soup

Shiitake mushrooms are a fabulous source of iron, and they also provide support to our immune and cardiovascular systems. Seek out mushrooms that are dry, plump, and clean for best quality and taste. Enjoy this creamy mushroom soup on a cold winter's day and melt all your worries away. Or, at least your worries about what to cook! After sautéing and simmering the vegetables, simply puree with coconut milk in a blender and you've got yourself a warming lunch or start to a delicious dinner.

2 cups sliced shiitake
    mushrooms

1 teaspoon salt

3 cups plus 3
    tablespoons water

1 small onion, chopped

1 stalk celery, chopped

1 large carrot, chopped

1 cup canned light
    coconut milk

2 tablespoons chopped
    scallions

Place the sliced shiitakes in a 2-quart saucepan along with the salt and the 3 tablespoons of water. Cook over medium-high heat until the mushrooms are softened and fragrant, about 5 minutes. Remove and reserve ¼ cup of the cooked mushrooms. Add the onion, celery, carrot, and the remaining 3 cups of water to the saucepan. Lower the heat to medium. Cook for 20 minutes, stirring occasionally. Allow to cool briefly, then place in a blender along with the canned coconut milk and blend until smooth. Serve hot and add about 1 tablespoon of the reserved mushrooms to each bowl of soup just before serving. Top with the scallions.

YIELD:

4 SERVINGS

PER SERVING:

89 CALORIES

3.2 G FAT

793 MG SODIUM

189 MG
POTASSIUM

16.9 G
CARBOHYDRATES

2.3 G PROTEIN

Carrot Rutabaga Butternut Bisque

Cashew milk yields a creamy result in this soup while still allowing the flavor of the vegetables to shine through. Rutabaga, a hearty root veggie that's high in potassium and vitamin C, may have originated as a cross between a turnip and cabbage.

1 cup peeled and cubed rutabaga

1 cup carrot coins

1 cup peeled, seeded, and cubed butternut squash

1 tablespoon freshly squeezed lemon juice

Salt

½ teaspoon sweet paprika

2 cups water

2 cups unsweetened Cashew Milk (page 133)

1 tablespoon coconut cream (optional; see page 9)

Preheat your oven to 400°F. Place the cubed rutabaga, carrot coins, and butternut squash on an ungreased cookie sheet and drizzle evenly with the lemon juice. Sprinkle with ¼ teaspoon of salt. Bake for 40 minutes, or until the vegetables are tender. Transfer the cooked vegetables to a blender or food processor and add the paprika and water. Blend until smooth and then stir in the cashew milk. Salt with ½ to ¾ teaspoon additional salt, to taste. Garnish with a drizzle of coconut cream, if desired, and serve warm. Store leftovers in an airtight container in the refrigerator for up to 4 days.

YIELD:

6 SERVINGS

PER SERVING:

165 CALORIES

11.2 G FAT

412 MG SODIUM

363 MG POTASSIUM

14 G CARBOHYDRATES

4.3 G PROTEIN

Cheesy Potato Soup

This soup is creamy, dreamy, cheesy, and extremely easy to pull together—especially if you have some raw cashews nuts already soaked and ready to go. If not, just toss 'em in a bowl, top with enough water to cover, and then wait a couple hours. After that, it just takes some boiling, smashing, a little pureeing, and voilà! instant comfort food. Make this soup even dreamier by adding a few slices of Portobello Bacon (page 181) right before serving.

8 cups vegan vegetable broth, such as Super Easy Veggie Broth (page 171)

5 Yukon gold potatoes, diced

2 cloves garlic, minced

1 onion, minced

1 sprig rosemary (in a cheesecloth sachet)

2 cups raw cashews, soaked in water for at least 2 hours and drained

¾ cup water

½ cup nutritional yeast

1 teaspoon salt, or to taste

3 to 4 scallions, chopped, for garnish

Freshly ground black pepper

In a large stockpot, combine the broth with the potatoes, garlic, onion, and rosemary sprig and bring to a boil over high heat. Once boiling, lower the heat to medium and let simmer for 30 minutes, or until the potatoes and onions are extremely well cooked.

In the meantime, combine the soaked cashews and the ¾ cup of water in a food processor and blend for about 8 minutes, or until very creamy, stopping and scraping down the sides of the bowl as needed.

Remove the rosemary sprig from the cooked potato mixture and then, using a potato masher, carefully mash about half of the cooked potatoes inside the pot. Whisk in the nutritional yeast and cashew cream until blended and add the salt. Garnish with chopped scallions and black pepper before serving.

YIELD:

10 SERVINGS

PER SERVING:

287 CALORIES

14.1 G FAT

817 MG SODIUM

905 MG POTASSIUM

30.1 G CARBOHYDRATES

13.7 G PROTEIN

Portobello Bacon

Use this tasty recipe to add a pop of flavor to so many different recipes. Sneak it in salads and wraps, use it on top of pizza, or my favorite, as an extra-special topping for Cheesy Potato Soup (page 180).

1 large or 2 medium-size portobello mushroom caps

¼ cup red wine vinegar

2 teaspoons liquid smoke

2 tablespoons pure maple syrup

¼ cup gluten-free soy sauce

1 tablespoon olive oil

1 teaspoon vegetable bouillon powder

Carefully remove the gills (the black ribs) from the mushroom cap, using a spoon, and slice the caps very thinly into twenty strips. Place the strips in a single layer in a small baking dish (about 8 x 8 inches).

In a small bowl, whisk together the remaining ingredients until very well blended. Pour evenly over the sliced mushrooms and marinate for 1 to 2 hours.

Preheat your oven to 300°F. Prepare a large cookie sheet by lining with a large sheet of parchment paper or a silicone mat. Carefully remove the individual mushroom slices and place on the prepared cookie sheet so that no strips are touching. Bake for 70 to 90 minutes, or until crispy, turning over halfway through cooking.

Use in your favorite recipes. Store in an airtight container in the refrigerator for up to 1 week.

YIELD:

8 SERVINGS

PER SERVING:

40 CALORIES

1.8 G FAT

477 MG SODIUM

108 MG POTASSIUM

5.1 G CARBOHYDRATES

1.3 G PROTEIN

New Potato Poppers

I call these delicious little guys "poppers" due to the way their paper-thin skin separates from the inside of the potatoes, making a fun *pop!* sound as you bite into each one. New potatoes can usually be located next to regular potatoes; you'll know them when you see them, as they look like tiny potatoes, generally no larger than 2 inches in diameter, and oftentimes as small as 1 inch.

24 ounces new potatoes (I like honey gold)

1 teaspoon avocado or olive oil

2 teaspoons ground cumin

1 teaspoon paprika

2 teaspoons fresh thyme

1 teaspoon salt

Preheat your oven to 425°F and line a large baking sheet with parchment paper. Scrub the new potatoes until clean and transfer to a medium-size bowl. Toss with the avocado oil to coat. In a small bowl, combine the cumin, paprika, thyme, and salt. Sprinkle evenly over the potatoes and toss well to coat the potatoes with the spice mixture.

Lay the coated potatoes in a single layer on the prepared baking sheet. Bake for 40 minutes, until the potatoes are tender and their skin is crispy. Enjoy immediately.

YIELD:

4 SERVINGS

PER SERVING:

126 CALORIES

0.7 G FAT

594 MG SODIUM

731 MG POTASSIUM

27.9 G CARBOHYDRATES

3.2 G PROTEIN

Delicata Squash Millet Bowl

Delicata squash has all the great features of a winter squash (flavorful, filling, slightly sweet) with none of the long cooking time or preparatory fuss of peeling and difficult slicing (I'm looking at you, pumpkin). Millet's sturdy texture pairs great with the silky-smooth sweetness of the delicata in this colorful dish that's great served warm or chilled.

1 delicata squash

½ teaspoon olive oil

¼ teaspoon salt

2 cups salted vegetable broth, such as Super Easy Veggie Broth (page 171)

1 cup uncooked millet

1 teaspoon garlic powder

½ teaspoon ground cumin

3 scallions, chopped

½ cup packed chopped fresh parsley

1 small red pepper, seeded and chopped

½ teaspoon freshly ground black pepper

Preheat your oven to 400°F and line a baking sheet with parchment paper. Slice the squash in half lengthwise, remove the seeds using a spoon, and then further slice the squash into ⅓-inch half-moon shapes. Arrange the squash on the prepared baking sheet in a single layer. Drizzle with the olive oil and sprinkle with the salt. Bake for 30 minutes, flipping halfway through cooking.

In a 2-quart saucepan, bring the vegetable broth to a boil over high heat. Add the millet, lower heat to low, and simmer for about 20 minutes, until the millet is tender and all the liquid is absorbed. Stir in the garlic powder and cumin. Toss with the scallions, parsley, and red pepper. Top with the delicata squash and black pepper and serve.

YIELD:

4 SERVINGS

PER SERVING:

245 CALORIES

3.5 G FAT

538 MG SODIUM

312 MG POTASSIUM

39.3 G CARBOHYDRATES

9.2 G PROTEIN

Delicata squash are considered winter squashes but they are much more perishable than a butternut or spaghetti squash. Store in the refrigerator after purchasing and use within 1 week for best flavor and texture.

Ricotta-Stuffed Creminis

An easy appetizer for a dinner party, these stuffed mushrooms are simple to throw together and the results seem as if you've spent all day on them. If you can't find creminis, large button mushrooms will work just as well.

10 cremini mushrooms, cleaned and stems removed

½ cup Brazil Nut Ricotta (page 137)

¼ cup packed chopped fresh cilantro

1 teaspoon olive oil

¼ teaspoon freshly ground black pepper

½ teaspoon salt

¼ cup Parmesan Sprinkles (page 138)

Preheat your oven to 375°F and line a small baking sheet with parchment paper. Place the mushrooms, top side down, snugly on the prepared baking sheet.

In a small bowl, mix the Brazil Nut Ricotta with the cilantro and stuff the mushroom caps full. Drizzle the caps with the oil and then sprinkle evenly with black pepper and salt and finally the Parmesan Sprinkles. Bake for 35 minutes, or until the mushrooms are tender. Serve hot.

YIELD:

10 SERVINGS

PER SERVING:

179 CALORIES

17 G FAT

248 MG SODIUM

279 MG POTASSIUM

4.8 G CARBOHYDRATES

5 G PROTEIN

Cucumber, Mango, and Radish Salad

When my young daughter first tried this salad, she delightfully squealed, "What are these red disks? They are beautiful and taste great!" This was the first time she had (knowingly) eaten a radish and I couldn't be more pleased with her reaction. If this is the first time you've enjoyed a radish, outside of a typical chain-restaurant house salad, I hope you feel similarly; it's a great starter radish recipe.

1 cup diced mango

1 small cucumber, thinly sliced (about 1 cup)

3 radishes, thinly sliced

¼ cup chopped radish greens

3 tablespoons freshly squeezed orange juice (mandarin is amazing here)

½ teaspoon salt

¼ teaspoon freshly ground black pepper

Place the mango, cucumber, radishes, and radish greens in a medium-size bowl and toss together to combine. In a small bowl, whisk together the orange juice, salt, and black pepper. Toss with the rest of the ingredients and then cover. Let rest in the refrigerator for 1 hour and up to 3 hours before serving. Serve chilled. Store in an airtight container for up to 2 days.

YIELD:

4 SERVINGS

PER SERVING:

54 CALORIES

0.2 G FAT

296 MG SODIUM

234 MG POTASSIUM

13 G CARBOHYDRATES

0.9 G PROTEIN

Roasted Radishes and Yellow Beets

This gorgeous duo makes a fun addition to a multiple course dinner or hearty lunch salad. Lightly seasoned with mustard and chives, these root veggies need little more than adequate roasting time to bring out their best.

10 radishes, most of greens removed

2 yellow beets, quartered (peeling is optional)

2 teaspoons stone-ground mustard

2 teaspoons olive oil

2 tablespoons chopped fresh chives

¼ teaspoon salt

Preheat your oven to 425°F. Scrub the radishes and beets and place in a large mixing bowl. In a small bowl, mix together the stone-ground mustard and olive oil and toss with the vegetables. Add the chives and toss to coat evenly. Arrange the radishes and beets in a single layer on an ungreased cookie sheet, sprinkle evenly with salt, and place on the center rack of the preheated oven. Bake for 30 minutes, or until the vegetables are fork-tender. Serve hot.

YIELD:

4 SERVINGS

PER SERVING:

46 CALORIES

2.5 G FAT

201 MG SODIUM

183 MG POTASSIUM

5.6 G CARBOHYDRATES

1 G PROTEIN

Cheesy Chili Sweet Potato Fries

There's a lot to love about these fries. Not only are they made with sweet potatoes, which boast a high amount of vitamin A and a decent amount of fiber, but they also require no frying! Therefore, they're simple to make, and as good for you as they are good to gobble up.

2 pounds sweet potatoes (about 2 large, long, tubular potatoes)

2 teaspoons coconut or olive oil

3 tablespoons Parmesan Sprinkles (page 138)

1 teaspoon ground chili seasoning, or to taste

½ teaspoon sweet paprika

Preheat your oven to 425°F. Peel the sweet potatoes, if you wish, and then slice into slender strips resembling French fries. The easiest way I've found to accomplish this is to first cut the sweet potato in half across and then slice the halves into three or four flat wedges. From there you can cut them into ½-inch-wide sticks. Transfer the sliced sweet potatoes to a large mixing bowl and toss with the coconut oil to coat.

In a small bowl, whisk together the Parmesan Sprinkles, chili seasoning, and paprika. Toss to coat the sweet potatoes and then arrange in a single layer on an ungreased baking sheet.

Bake for 15 minutes, flip, and bake for an additional 15 minutes. Turn off the oven and crack the door open ever so slightly. Let the sweet potatoes remain in the oven for about 25 minutes, or until crispy. Serve hot with your favorite dipping sauce.

YIELD:

6 SERVINGS

PER SERVING:

210 CALORIES

3.3 G FAT

212 MG SODIUM

1268 MG POTASSIUM

43.1 G CARBOHYDRATES

3 G PROTEIN

Glazed Baby Carrots

This dish is a wonderful recipe to make during the holidays, or when you're craving something fancy with very little fuss. If you can, seek out true baby carrots, small carrots that are harvested in the early stages of growth with the greens still attached, rather than prepackaged carrots that have been shaped into "baby" bites. The greens add a lovely addition to the presentation and they have a nice flavor, too.

About 20 baby carrots

2 teaspoons salt

2⅓ cups water

3 tablespoons pure
    maple syrup

In a small skillet, place the carrots in a single layer and salt evenly with 1 teaspoon of the salt. Add 2 cups of the water to cover and bring to a boil over medium-high heat. Lower the heat slightly, so that the carrots remain at a boil, and cook for 5 minutes. Drain and return to the pan, along with the maple syrup, remaining teaspoon of salt, and remaining ⅓ cup of water. Cook over medium-low heat for about 7 minutes, or until the sauce has reduced by at least half.

Serve hot.

YIELD:

4 SERVINGS

PER SERVING:

64 CALORIES

0 G FAT

978 MG SODIUM

222 MG
POTASSIUM

15.9 G
CARBOHYDRATES

0.5 G PROTEIN

Ravishing Red Slaw

A fun twist on traditional coleslaw, this recipe features a few of my favorite veggies that combine beautifully to create a crimson slaw that's tasty and stunning. I find this side tastes best if the flavors have time to meld, so I recommend letting it rest overnight before enjoying. Red cabbage is bursting with a type of phytochemical called polyphenols (and in a much greater amount than green cabbage), which are thought to have both antioxidant and anticancer effects.

3 cups shredded red cabbage

2 carrots, shredded

1 medium-size beet, peeled and shredded

2 tablespoons cider vinegar

2 tablespoons pure maple syrup

3 tablespoons Stealthy Healthy Mayo (page 139) or other light vegan mayo

⅛ teaspoon salt

Place the shredded cabbage, carrots, and beet in a medium-size to large bowl. Toss with the cider vinegar and allow to rest 15 minutes. Stir in the maple syrup, mayo, and salt and mix well to combine. Place in the refrigerator and allow to rest for at least 2 hours up to overnight before serving. Store in an airtight container for up to 4 days.

YIELD:

4 SERVINGS

PER SERVING:

91 CALORIES

2.7 G FAT

207 MG SODIUM

289 MG POTASSIUM

16.1 G CARBOHYDRATES

1.3 G PROTEIN

Jicama and Beet Green Frittata

Jicama (pronounced: *heek-a-muh* and also known as "Mexican yam") is a root vegetable that has a crisp texture and mellow flavor similar to a less starchy parsnip or carrot. Often enjoyed raw, it turns quite tender when cooked, adding a lovely texture to this egg-free frittata.

1 cup chickpea flour

1 cup water

1 tablespoon olive oil

1½ teaspoons salt

1 teaspoon ground coriander

1 teaspoon baking powder

1 (14-ounce) block extra-firm tofu, drained and pressed gently

1 clove garlic, minced

¾ teaspoon orange zest (optional)

1 cup chopped beet greens and stems

1 cup peeled and diced (½-inch) jicama

1 shallot or ½ small red onion, thinly sliced

Preheat your oven to 350°F and lightly grease a standard-size glass pie pan. In a medium-size bowl, whisk together the chickpea flour and water until smooth. Add the olive oil, 1 teaspoon of the salt, and the coriander and baking powder and mix well. Crumble the tofu on top of the chickpea flour batter and sprinkle lightly with the remaining ½ teaspoon of salt. Stir well to combine. Fold in the garlic; orange zest, if using; beet greens; and jicama and spread in the prepared pie pan. Top evenly with the sliced shallot. Bake, uncovered, for 65 to 70 minutes, or until deep golden in color and quite firm.

Let cool for at least 15 to 20 minutes before serving. Best if eaten at room temperature, or just slightly warm.

YIELD:

8 SERVINGS

PER SERVING:

130 CALORIES

3.4 G FAT

462 MG SODIUM

410 MG POTASSIUM

17.9 G CARBOHYDRATES

8.7 G PROTEIN

Carrot Cake Smoothie

Leave the carrots in this recipe unpeeled for an extra-nutritional boost. Most of the nutrients in a carrot are said to be found in the skin and directly beneath it, so in this case, it's a virtue to take the easy route with prep: Simply scrub the carrots clean and toss them in the blender. I even leave about 2 inches of the greens still attached, and it still tastes great!

3 average-size carrots, unpeeled (about 1 cup chopped)

1 small red apple (I like Honeycrisp and Gala), skin on, cored

1 average-size banana, peeled and frozen

2 tablespoons blackstrap molasses

¼ cup coarsely chopped pecans

Pinch of freshly grated nutmeg

Pinch of ground cloves

1 teaspoon ground cinnamon

½ teaspoon pure vanilla extract

2 cups unsweetened almond milk

Place all the ingredients in a blender and blend until very smooth, stopping and scraping down the sides of the blender container as needed. Serve immediately.

YIELD:

2 SERVINGS

PER SERVING:

298 CALORIES

6.1 G FAT

150 MG SODIUM

1202 MG POTASSIUM

55 G CARBOHYDRATES

10 G PROTEIN

Half and Half Marinara Sauce

This sauce is called "half and half" because it's made with half tomato and half butternut squash! The squash imparts a delicate sweetness to the sauce while lending it a smooth texture not unlike that of slow-cooked tomatoes. If you're not a fan of raw garlic (it can be a bit zippy), feel free to roast the garlic alongside the butternut squash by simply peeling and placing in a foil pouch, then toss into the blender as directed.

1 average-size butternut squash

1⅛ teaspoons salt

2 (6-ounce) cans tomato paste

2 heaping teaspoons Italian seasoning

2 cloves garlic

2 tablespoons balsamic vinegar

2 cups water

Preheat your oven to 350°F. Slice the butternut squash in half and remove the seeds. Sprinkle the fleshy sides of the squash with the ⅛ teaspoon of salt and then place, face down, on a rimmed baking sheet. Add ¼ cup water to the bottom of the sheet. Place carefully in the preheated oven and bake for about 1 hour, or until the skin of the squash can easily be pierced with a fork. Remove from the oven and scoop the cooked squash from the skin.

Place in a blender along with the rest of the ingredients, including the remaining teaspoon of salt, and puree until smooth, making sure to stop and scrape down the sides of the blender container often.

Use immediately or store in an airtight container in the refrigerator for up to 5 days.

YIELD:

4 SERVINGS

PER SERVING:

112 CALORIES

1.2 G FAT

746 MG SODIUM

1123 MG POTASSIUM

25.1 G CARBOHYDRATES

4.5 G PROTEIN

RECIPE PAIRING SUGGESTIONS

In need of some meal ideas or pairings for the small plates in this book? You've come to the right page! Here are some suggestions of recipes that pair well for great flavor and a good balance of essential nutrients; add a small bowl of greens or some fresh fruit or vegetable slices for delicious, filling meals. Enjoy these combos as suggested, or mix them up to match your own personal tastes!

Curried Collard Wraps (page 21) + Cheesy Chili Sweet Potato Fries (page 191)

Red Quinoa Tabbouleh (page 54) + Rainbow Veggie Chili (page 147)

Sweet Mustard–Glazed Rapini (page 35) + Not-So-Dirty Rice (page 51)

Kabocha, Apple, and Fennel Bisque (page 79) + Pecan-Stuffed Okra (page 114)

Popcorn Tofu (page 145) + Beyond Good BBQ Sauce (page 101) + Cucumber, Mango, and Radish Salad (page 187)

Brilliant Beet Soup (page 174) + Roasted Grape and Asparagus Salad (page 75)

New Potato Poppers (page 182) + Spaghetti Squash with Broccoli and Button Mushrooms (page 173)

Jicama and Beet Green Frittata (page 196) + Serious Taco Salad (page 19)

Sweet Potato Cauliflower Soup (page 175) + Dilly Avocado Toasts (page 76)

Flax and Chia Garlic Crackers (page 116) + Pizza Hummus (page 158) + Roasted Corn and Cilantro Chili (page 149)

Cheesy Potato Soup (page 180) + Portobello Bacon (page 181) + Power Up Kale Salad (page 27)

Yukon-Stuffed Poblanos (page 164) + Summertime Quinoa Bowl (page 57)

Garlicky Rainbow Chard and Cannellinis (page 31) + Wild Rice Pilaf (Page 53)

Zucchini-Laced Fusilli (page 167) + Ravishing Red Slaw (page 195)

Avocado Chick'n Salad (page 146) + Carrot Rutabaga Butternut Bisque (page 179)

Delicata Squash Millet Bowl (page 183) + Cream of Shiitake Soup (page 176)

Get Up and Go Granola (page 58) + Blueberries and Cream Mousse (page 98)

Magnificent Mushroom Pizza (page 168) + Pesto Haricots Verts (page 156)

Rustic Ratatouille (page 170) + Red Bean Sweet Potato Salad (page 152)

Crispy Baked Falafel (page 142) + White Bean Ranch Dressing (page 161) + Roasted Radishes and Yellow Beets (page 188)

Mighty Mac and Collards (page 20) + Oil-Free Roasted Broccoli (page 34)

Vanilla Almond Granola (page 120) + Cashew Milk (page 133) + Kiwi Salad (page 86)

METRIC CONVERSIONS

- The recipes in this book have not been tested with metric measurements, so some variations might occur.

- Remember that the weight of dry ingredients varies according to the volume or density factor: 1 cup of flour weighs far less than 1 cup of sugar, and 1 tablespoon doesn't necessarily hold 3 teaspoons.

GENERAL FORMULA FOR METRIC CONVERSION

Ounces to grams	ounces × 28.35 = grams
Grams to ounces	grams × 0.035 = ounces
Pounds to grams	pounds × 453.5 = grams
Pounds to kilograms	pounds × 0.45 = kilograms
Cups to liters	cups × 0.24 = liters
Fahrenheit to Celsius	(°F – 32) × 5 ÷ 9 = °C
Celsius to Fahrenheit	(°C × 9) ÷ 5 + 32 = °F

VOLUME (LIQUID) MEASUREMENTS

1 teaspoon = ⅙ fluid ounce = 5 milliliters

1 tablespoon = ½ fluid ounce = 15 milliliters

2 tablespoons = 1 fluid ounce = 30 milliliters

¼ cup = 2 fluid ounces = 60 milliliters

⅓ cup = 2⅔ fluid ounces = 79 milliliters

½ cup = 4 fluid ounces = 118 milliliters

1 cup or ½ pint = 8 fluid ounces = 250 milliliters

2 cups or 1 pint = 16 fluid ounces = 500 milliliters

4 cups or 1 quart = 32 fluid ounces = 1,000 milliliters

1 gallon = 4 liters

VOLUME (DRY) MEASUREMENTS

¼ teaspoon = 1 milliliter

½ teaspoon = 2 milliliters

¾ teaspoon = 4 milliliters

1 teaspoon = 5 milliliters

1 tablespoon = 15 milliliters

¼ cup = 59 milliliters

⅓ cup = 79 milliliters

½ cup = 118 milliliters

⅔ cup = 158 milliliters

¾ cup = 177 milliliters

1 cup = 225 milliliters

4 cups or 1 quart = 1 liter

½ gallon = 2 liters

1 gallon = 4 liters

OVEN TEMPERATURE EQUIVALENTS, FAHRENHEIT (F) AND CELSIUS (C)

100°F = 38°C

200°F = 95°C

250°F = 120°C

300°F = 150°C

350°F = 180°C

400°F = 205°C

450°F = 230°C

WEIGHT (MASS) MEASUREMENTS

1 ounce = 30 grams

2 ounces = 55 grams

3 ounces = 85 grams

4 ounces = ¼ pound = 125 grams

8 ounces = ½ pound = 240 grams

12 ounces = ¾ pound = 375 grams

16 ounces = 1 pound = 454 grams

LINEAR MEASUREMENTS

½ in = 1½ cm

1 inch = 2½ cm

6 inches = 15 cm

8 inches = 20 cm

10 inches = 25 cm

12 inches = 30 cm

20 inches = 50 cm

ACKNOWLEDGMENTS

So many thanks to give:

To J. D. Kramer, my amazing husband, who always has the best (most constructive!) things to say about my work, thank you for always being there and for always being so supportive. Landen and Olive, you guys, too. I'm so lucky to have such an awesome family.

To Sally Ekus, Lisa Ekus, Jaimee Constantine, and the rest of the gang at TLEG, thank you—again and again for everything you've done over the years and for all you've done on this book. I am proud to be represented by such an incredible literary agency.

Renée Sedliar and Claire Ivett, thank for your tremendous edits and all the hard work you put towards this manuscript. Thanks also to everyone else at Da Capo Lifelong Books for making this book come to life.

To all my readers, near and far, thank you for making yet another book possible. I am so grateful for your readership and inspiration.

Laurel Vanblarcum, thank you for your time and consideration with the initial edits of the manuscript—your input, as always, is so very helpful. To my recipe testers, Jim Allen, Dianne Wenz, Jenni Mischel, Ines Lopes, Lauren McPhee, Nicolle Picou Thomas, Racine Verworlf, Unice Sanford, Anna Cordova, Jennifer Wade, Sonia Lemoine, Lisa Angerame, Lisa Maria Garcia, and Veronique Daoust—thank you all so so so much. You all were instrumental in making these recipes ready for the world. I'm incredibly grateful to have had all your help!

ABOUT THE AUTHOR

Allyson Kramer is a cookbook author, food
photographer, and visual artist living in
Philadelphia. She is passionate about nu-
trition and fitness and has been creating
plant-based recipes for over twenty years.
Kramer's work has been featured in *Easy Eats
Magazine*, *Vegetarian Times*, the Huffington
Post, and more.

INDEX

A

ACV Fizz, 105

almond butter

Caramel Pepita Cookies, 125

Choco-Chip, PB & Banana Oatmeal (a.k.a My Favorite Oatmeal), 50

Simple Soft and Chewy Granola Bars, 117

almond meal

Almond-Roasted Romanesco, 33

Cherry Almond Millet, 61

Chocolate Cheesecake, 126

Cinnamon Plum Streusel, 93

Oil-Free Hummus, 157

Parmesan Sprinkles, 138

Popcorn Tofu, 145

Simple Soft and Chewy Granola Bars, 117

Vanilla Almond Granola, 120

almond milk

Almond Milk, homemade, 134

Carrot Applesauce Muffins, 91

Carrot Cake Smoothie, 197

Cherry Almond Millet, 61

Chocolate Gooseberry Pudding, 95

Cinnamon Bun Milk Shake, 65

Easy as Sunday Morning Banana Pancakes, 92

Goji Overnight Oats, 48

Insanely Addictive Queso, 111

Lemony Lime Chia Pudding, 88

Mint Chocolate Chip Smoothie, 42

Three-Grain Breakfast Medley, 47

Almond-Roasted Romanesco, 33

almonds

Almond Milk, 134

Chocolate Hazelnut Bites, 129

apple cider

Apple-Infused Shredded Brussels, 32

apple cider vinegar

ACV Fizz, 105

Apple-Infused Shredded Brussels, 32

apples

Caramel Apple Parfaits, 96

Carrot Cake Smoothie, 197

Kabocha, Apple, and Fennel Bisque, 79

applesauce

Carrot Applesauce Muffins, 91

artichokes

Spinach Artichoke Dip, 36

arugula

Walnut Arugula Pesto, 43

asparagus

Light and Lemony Fusilli with Asparagus and Roasted Tomatoes, 72

Roasted Grape and Asparagus Salad, 75

avocados

Avocado Chick'n Salad, 146

Chocolate Gelato, 127

Dilly Avocado Toasts, 76

Greenest Goddess Dressing, 44

Sun-Dried Tomato Guacamole, 82

B

baking sheets and pans, 13

bananas

Banana Oatmeal Raisin Cookies, 66

Carrot Cake Smoothie, 197

Choco-Chip, PB & Banana Oatmeal (a.k.a My Favorite Oatmeal), 50

Chocolate Brownie Cake, 69

Cinnamon Bun Milk Shake, 65

Easy as Sunday Morning Banana Pancakes, 92

Hunky Monkey Ice Cream, 97

Mint Chocolate Chip Smoothie, 42

Strawberry Banana Green Smoothie, 40

bars

Chewy Cherry Chia Bars, 118

Cocoa Carob Bars, 119

Simple Soft and Chewy Granola Bars, 117

beans

about, 7–8

Garlicky Rainbow Chard and Cannellinis, 31

Peanut Butter Black Bean Brownie Bites, 159

Pesto Haricots Verts, 156

Plantain Tacos, 81

Rainbow Veggie Chili, 147

Red Bean Sweet Potato Salad, 152

Roasted Corn and Cilantro Chili, 149

Serious Taco Salad, 19

White Bean Ranch Dressing, 161

Zesty Black Bean Soup, 148

beans, refried

Roasted Corn and Cilantro Chili, 149

beet greens

Jicama and Beet Green Frittata, 196

beets
- Brilliant Beet Soup, 174
- Ravishing Red Slaw, 195
- Roasted Radishes and Yellow Beets, 188

besan. *See chickpea flour*

beverages
- ACV Fizz, 105
- Almond Milk, 134
- Cashew Milk, 133
- Cinnamon Bun Milk Shake, 65
- Rosemary Cucumber Cooler, 106

Beyond Good BBQ Sauce, 101

Blackberry Coconut Quinoa, 60

blenders, 13

blueberries
- Blackberry Coconut Quinoa, 60
- Blueberries and Cream Mousse, 98
- Wild Rice Pilaf, 53

Brazil nuts
- Brazil Nut Ricotta, 137
- Ricotta-Stuffed Creminis, 184

breads
- Carrot Applesauce Muffins, 91
- Chocolate Teff Waffles, 62
- Cinnamon Pumpkin Donuts, 63
- Dilly Avocado Toasts, 76
- Easy as Sunday Morning Banana Pancakes, 92
- Flax and Chia Garlic Crackers, 116
- Lighten Up Pizza Crust, 160

breakfast
- Choco-Chip, PB & Banana Oatmeal (a.k.a My Favorite Oatmeal), 50
- Cinnamon Bun Milk Shake, 65
- Cinnamon Pumpkin Donuts, 63
- Dilly Avocado Toasts, 76
- Easy as Sunday Morning Banana Pancakes, 92
- Get Up and Go Granola, 58
- Goji Overnight Oats, 48
- Lemony Lime Chia Pudding, 88
- Sunshine Breakfast UnScramble, 150
- Three-Grain Breakfast Medley, 47
- Vanilla Almond Granola, 120

Brilliant Beet Soup, 174

broccoli
- Oil-Free Roasted Broccoli, 34
- Spaghetti Squash with Broccoli and Button Mushrooms, 173
- Sunshine Breakfast UnScramble, 150

broccoli rabe. *See rapini*

brown rice flour
- about, 12–13
- Chocolate Gooseberry Pudding, 95
- Easy as Sunday Morning Banana Pancakes, 92
- Lighten Up Pizza Crust, 160

Brussels sprouts
- Apple-Infused Shredded Brussels, 32

buckwheat flour
- about, 8
- Carrot Applesauce Muffins, 91
- Cinnamon Pumpkin Donuts, 63

C

cabbage
- Easy Kimchi, 24–25
- Korean Napa Tacos, 22
- Ravishing Red Slaw, 195

cacao butter
- about, 8
- Chocolate-Covered Hemp Cookies, 124
- Too Good for You to Be True Chocolate, 128
- White Chocolate Peanut Butter Fudge Bites, 130

cacao nibs
- Choco-Chip, PB & Banana Oatmeal (a.k.a My Favorite Oatmeal), 50
- Chocolate-Covered Hemp Cookies, 124
- Hunky Monkey Ice Cream, 97

candy
- candy molds, 13
- White Chocolate Peanut Butter Fudge Bites, 130

Cantaloupe Mango Sorbet, 99

Caramel Apple Parfaits, 96

Caramel Pepita Cookies, 125

Cardamom Orange Ice, 100

carob flour
- Cocoa Carob Bars, 119

carob powder, about, 8–9

carrots
- Carrot Applesauce Muffins, 91
- Carrot Cake Smoothie, 197
- Carrot Rutabaga Butternut Bisque, 179
- Flax and Chia Garlic Crackers, 116
- Glazed Baby Carrots, 192
- Ravishing Red Slaw, 195
- Rustic Ratatouille, 170
- Super Easy Veggie Broth, 171

cashews, raw
- about, 10, 12
- Caramel Apple Parfaits, 96
- Cashew Milk, homemade, 133
- Cheesy Potato Soup, 180
- Chewy Cherry Chia Bars, 118
- Chocolate Cheesecake, 126
- Chocolate-Covered Hemp Cookies, 124
- Cocoa Carob Bars, 119
- Creamy Cashew Cheese, 136
- Creamy Tomato Bisque, 80
- Insanely Addictive Queso, 111

Nutty Butter Cookies, 123

Simple Cashew Cream, 135

Spinach Artichoke Dip, 36

Stealthy Healthy Mayo, 139

Zucchini-Laced Fusilli, 167

cauliflower

Sweet Potato Cauliflower Soup, 175

chard

Garlicky Rainbow Chard and
Cannellinis, 31

Cheesy BBQ Kale Chips, 39

Cheesy Chili Sweet Potato Fries, 191

Cheesy Potato Soup, 180

cheese graters, 13–14

cherries

Cherry Almond Millet, 61

Chewy Cherry Chia Bars, 118

Get Up and Go Granola, 58

chia seeds

about, 9

Chewy Cherry Chia Bars, 118

Chocolate-Covered Hemp Cookies,
124

Cinnamon Pumpkin Donuts, 63

Flax and Chia Garlic Crackers, 116

Get Up and Go Granola, 58

Lemony Lime Chia Pudding, 88

Oil-Free Hummus, 157

Simple Soft and Chewy Granola
Bars, 117

chickpea flour

about, 8

Carrot Applesauce Muffins, 91

Chocolate Brownie Cake, 69

Chocolate Gooseberry Pudding, 95

Cinnamon Plum Streusel, 93

Cinnamon Pumpkin Donuts, 63

Crispy Baked Falafel, 142–143

Jicama and Beet Green Frittata, 196

Lighten Up Pizza Crust, 160

Popcorn Tofu, 145

Rainbow Veggie Chili, 147

Sunshine Breakfast UnScramble, 150

chickpeas

Avocado Chick'n Salad, 146

Crispy Baked Falafel, 142–143

Light and Lemony Fusilli with
Asparagus and Roasted Tomatoes,
72

Oil-Free Hummus, 157

Pizza Hummus, 158

chocolate

Choco-Chip, PB & Banana Oatmeal
(a.k.a My Favorite Oatmeal), 50

Chocolate Brownie Cake, 69

Chocolate Cheesecake, 126

Chocolate-Covered Hemp Cookies,
124

Chocolate Gelato, 127

Chocolate Gooseberry Pudding, 95

Chocolate Hazelnut Bites, 129

Chocolate Teff Waffles, 62

Oh-So-Rich Chocolate Glaze, 70

Too Good for You to Be True
Chocolate, 128

*See also cacao butter; cacao nibs;
carob flour; cocoa powder*

Cinnamon Bun Milk Shake, 65

Cinnamon Plum Streusel, 93

Cinnamon Pumpkin Donuts, 63

cocoa butter. *See cacao butter*

cocoa powder

about, 9

Chocolate Brownie Cake, 69

Chocolate Cheesecake, 126

Chocolate-Covered Hemp Cookies,
124

Chocolate Gelato, 127

Chocolate Gooseberry Pudding, 95

Chocolate Hazelnut Bites, 129

Chocolate Teff Waffles, 62

Cocoa Carob Bars, 119

Mint Chocolate Chip Smoothie, 42

Oh-So-Rich Chocolate Glaze, 70

Peanut Butter Black Bean Brownie
Bites, 159

Too Good for You to Be True
Chocolate, 128

coconut chips

Blackberry Coconut Quinoa, 60

coconut cream

about, 9

Kiwi Salad, 86

coconut milk

Chocolate Gelato, 127

Cream of Shiitake Soup, 176

Simple Cashew Cream, 135

Thai Peanut Dressing, 113

collards

Curried Collard Wraps, 21

Mighty Mac and Collards, 20

Rainbow Veggie Chili, 147

Super Easy Veggie Broth, 171

cookies

Banana Oatmeal Raisin Cookies, 66

Caramel Pepita Cookies, 125

Chocolate-Covered Hemp Cookies,
124

Chocolate Hazelnut Bites, 129

Nutty Butter Cookies, 123

corn

Rainbow Veggie Chili, 147

Red Bean Sweet Potato Salad, 152

Roasted Corn and Cilantro Chili, 149

Cream of Shiitake Soup, 176

Creamy Cashew Cheese, 136

Creamy Tomato Bisque, 80

Crispy Baked Falafel, 142–143

cucumbers

Cucumber, Mango, and Radish Salad, 187

Rosemary Cucumber Cooler, 106

Curried Collard Wraps, 21

cutting boards, 14

D

dates

Blueberries and Cream Mousse, 98

Cantaloupe Mango Sorbet, 99

Caramel Apple Parfaits, 96

Caramel Pepita Cookies, 125

Chewy Cherry Chia Bars, 118

Chocolate Cheesecake, 126

Chocolate-Covered Hemp Cookies, 124

Chocolate Gelato, 127

Chocolate Hazelnut Bites, 129

Cinnamon Bun Milk Shake, 65

Cocoa Carob Bars, 119

Mint Chocolate Chip Smoothie, 42

Nutty Butter Cookies, 123

Strawberry Banana Green Smoothie, 40

Delicata Squash Millet Bowl, 183

desserts

Blueberries and Cream Mousse, 98

Cantaloupe Mango Sorbet, 99

Caramel Apple Parfaits, 96

Cardamom Orange Ice, 100

Chocolate Brownie Cake, 69

Chocolate Cheesecake, 126

Chocolate Gelato, 127

Chocolate Gooseberry Pudding, 95

Cinnamon Bun Milk Shake, 65

Cinnamon Plum Streusel, 93

Cinnamon Pumpkin Donuts, 63

Hunky Monkey Ice Cream, 97

Oh-So-Rich Chocolate Glaze, 70

Peanut Butter Black Bean Brownie Bites, 159

Roasted Pears with Walnuts, 94

Too Good for You to Be True Chocolate, 128

Dilly Avocado Toasts, 76

dips

Spinach Artichoke Dip, 36

Sun-Dried Tomato Guacamole, 82

Superfresh Salsa, 83

Walnut Eggplant Dip, 115

donut pans, 63

Dried Fruit Salad, 87

E

Easy as Sunday Morning Banana Pancakes, 92

Easy Kimchi, 24–25

eggplant

Rustic Ratatouille, 170

Walnut Eggplant Dip, 115

exercise, 7

F

FDA (Food and Drug Administration), 3

fennel

Kabocha, Apple, and Fennel Bisque, 79

filberts

Chocolate Hazelnut Bites, 129

flaxseeds

about, 10

Cinnamon Bun Milk Shake, 65

Flax and Chia Garlic Crackers, 116

Goji Overnight Oats, 48

flour. *See brown rice flour; buckwheat flour; carob flour; chickpea flour; peanut flour; sorghum flour; teff flour*

food choices, effect of on mental and physical health, 1–2

food processors, 14

fruit, dried

Get Up and Go Granola, 58

G

garbanzo bean flour. *See chickpea flour*

Garlicky Rainbow Chard and Cannellinis, 31

Get Up and Go Granola, 58

Glazed Baby Carrots, 192

goji berries

about, 9–10

Dried Fruit Salad, 87

Get Up and Go Granola, 58

Goji Overnight Oats, 48

gooseberries

Chocolate Gooseberry Pudding, 95

grapes

Avocado Chick'n Salad, 146

Roasted Grape and Asparagus Salad, 75

graters, 13–14

Greenest Goddess Dressing, 44

greens, about, 5

Guacamole, Sun-Dried Tomato, 82

H

Half and Half Marinara Sauce, 198

hazelnuts

Chocolate Hazelnut Bites, 129

hemp hearts

about, 10

Chocolate-Covered Hemp Cookies, 124

Simple Soft and Chewy Granola Bars, 117

Hunky Monkey Ice Cream, 97

I

ice-cream makers, 14

Insanely Addictive Queso, 111

J

Jicama and Beet Green Frittata, 196

K

Kabocha, Apple, and Fennel Bisque, 79

kale

Cheesy BBQ Kale Chips, 39

Power Up Kale Salad, 27

Serious Taco Salad, 19

Strawberry Banana Green Smoothie, 40

Super Easy Veggie Broth, 171

kasha

Three-Grain Breakfast Medley, 47

Kimchi, Easy, 24–25

Kiwi Salad, 86

knives, 14

Korean Napa Tacos, 22

L

lemons

Lemony Lime Chia Pudding, 88

Light and Lemony Fusilli with Asparagus and Roasted Tomatoes, 72

Parmesan Sprinkles, 138

Rosemary Cucumber Cooler, 106

lentils

Orange Lentil Salad, 153

Light and Lemony Fusilli with Asparagus and Roasted Tomatoes, 72

Lighten Up Pizza Crust, 160

limes

Brazil Nut Ricotta, 137

Lemony Lime Chia Pudding, 88

M

macadamia nuts

Nutty Butter Cookies, 123

Magnificent Mushroom Pizza, 168

mandolines, 15

mangos

Cantaloupe Mango Sorbet, 99

Cucumber, Mango, and Radish Salad, 187

Mighty Mac and Collards, 20

millet

Cherry Almond Millet, 61

Delicata Squash Millet Bowl, 183

Three-Grain Breakfast Medley, 47

mint

Mint Chocolate Chip Smoothie, 42

Minted Watermelon Salad, 85

mulberries, dried

Dried Fruit Salad, 87

mushrooms

Cream of Shiitake Soup, 176

Magnificent Mushroom Pizza, 168

Pad Thai Soba Noodles, 112

Portobello Bacon, 181

Ricotta-Stuffed Creminis, 184

Spaghetti Squash with Broccoli and Button Mushrooms, 173

Super Easy Veggie Broth, 171

Zesty Black Bean Soup, 148

N

New Potato Poppers, 182

noodles, buckwheat soba

Pad Thai Soba Noodles, 112

Not-So-Dirty Rice, 51

nuts

Caramel Apple Parfaits, 96

Chocolate Hazelnut Bites, 129

Cocoa Carob Bars, 119

Hunky Monkey Ice Cream, 97

Nutty Butter Cookies, 123

Ricotta-Stuffed Creminis, 184

Roasted Pears with Walnuts, 94

Vanilla Almond Granola, 120

See also almond butter; almond meal; cashews, raw; peanut butter; specific nuts

Nutty Butter Cookies, 123

O

oats

Banana Oatmeal Raisin Cookies, 66

Chewy Cherry Chia Bars, 118

Choco-Chip, PB & Banana Oatmeal (a.k.a My Favorite Oatmeal), 50

Cinnamon Bun Milk Shake, 65

Cinnamon Plum Streusel, 93

Dried Fruit Salad, 87

Get Up and Go Granola, 58

Goji Overnight Oats, 48

Simple Soft and Chewy Granola Bars, 117

Vanilla Almond Granola, 120

Oh-So-Rich Chocolate Glaze, 70

Oil-Free Hummus, 157

Oil-Free Roasted Broccoli, 34

okra

Pecan-Stuffed Okra, 114

oranges

Cardamom Orange Ice, 100

Orange Lentil Salad, 153

P

Pad Thai Soba Noodles, 112

Papaya Salad, 84

parchment paper, 15

Parmesan Sprinkles, 138

pasta
  Light and Lemony Fusilli with Asparagus and Roasted Tomatoes, 72
  Mighty Mac and Collards, 20
  Pad Thai Soba Noodles, 112
  Zucchini-Laced Fusilli, 167
peanut butter
  Choco-Chip, PB & Banana Oatmeal (a.k.a My Favorite Oatmeal), 50
  Pad Thai Soba Noodles, 112
  Peanut Butter Black Bean Brownie Bites, 159
  Thai Peanut Dressing, 113
  White Chocolate Peanut Butter Fudge Bites, 130
peanut flour
  about, 10
  Nutty Butter Cookies, 123
pears
  Roasted Pears with Walnuts, 94
pecans
  Cocoa Carob Bars, 119
  Pecan-Stuffed Okra, 114
pepitas
  Caramel Pepita Cookies, 125
  Dried Fruit Salad, 87
peppers, bell
  Insanely Addictive Queso, 111
  Pad Thai Soba Noodles, 112
  Rainbow Veggie Chili, 147
  Roasted Corn and Cilantro Chili, 149
  Superfresh Salsa, 83
  Zesty Black Bean Soup, 148
peppers, chile
  Not-So-Dirty Rice, 51
  Superfresh Salsa, 83
  Yukon-Stuffed Poblanos, 164
  Zesty Black Bean Soup, 148
Pesto Haricots Verts, 156

pineapple juice
  Tempeh and Snow Peas, 155
Pizza Hummus, 158
Plantain Tacos, 81
plums
  Cinnamon Plum Streusel, 93
pomegranate arils
  Blackberry Coconut Quinoa, 60
Popcorn Tofu, 145
Portobello Bacon, 181
potatoes
  Cheesy Potato Soup, 180
  New Potato Poppers, 182
  Rainbow Veggie Chili, 147
  Red Potato Watercress Salad, 28
  Yukon-Stuffed Poblanos, 164
Power Up Kale Salad, 27
pumpkin
  Cinnamon Pumpkin Donuts, 63
pumpkin seeds. See pepitas

Q

Queso, Insanely Addictive, 111
quinoa
  Blackberry Coconut Quinoa, 60
  Red Quinoa Tabbouleh, 54
  Summertime Quinoa Bowl, 57
  Three-Grain Breakfast Medley, 47

R

raab. See rapini
radishes
  Cucumber, Mango, and Radish Salad, 187
  Roasted Radishes and Yellow Beets, 188
Rainbow Veggie Chili, 147

raisins
  Banana Oatmeal Raisin Cookies, 66
  Dried Fruit Salad, 87
  Get Up and Go Granola, 58
  Zucchini-Laced Fusilli, 167
rapini
  Sweet Mustard-Glazed Rapini, 35
Raspberry Vinaigrette, 102
Ravishing Red Slaw, 195
Red Bean Sweet Potato Salad, 152
Red Potato Watercress Salad, 28
Red Quinoa Tabbouleh, 54
rice
  Mighty Mac and Collards, 20
  Not-So-Dirty Rice, 51
  Wild Rice Pilaf, 53
rice cookers, 15
rice flour. See brown rice flour
Ricotta-Stuffed Creminis, 184
Roasted Corn and Cilantro Chili, 149
Roasted Grape and Asparagus Salad, 75
Roasted Pears with Walnuts, 94
Roasted Radishes and Yellow Beets, 188
romanesco
  Almond-Roasted Romanesco, 33
Rosemary Cucumber Cooler, 106
Rustic Ratatouille, 170
rutabagas
  Carrot Rutabaga Butternut Bisque, 179

S

salad dressings
  Greenest Goddess Dressing, 44
  Raspberry Vinaigrette, 102
  Thai Peanut Dressing, 113
  White Bean Ranch Dressing, 161

salads
  Avocado Chick'n Salad, 146
  Cucumber, Mango, and Radish Salad, 187
  Kiwi Salad, 86
  Minted Watermelon Salad, 85
  Orange Lentil Salad, 153
  Papaya Salad, 84
  Power Up Kale Salad, 27
  Red Bean Sweet Potato Salad, 152
  Red Potato Watercress Salad, 28
  Roasted Grape and Asparagus Salad, 75
  Serious Taco Salad, 19
  Wakame Salad, 23
sauces
  Beyond Good BBQ Sauce, 101
  Half and Half Marinara Sauce, 198
  Thai Peanut Dressing, 113
Serious Taco Salad, 19
silicone mats, 15
Simple Cashew Cream, 135
Simple Soft and Chewy Granola Bars, 117
smoothies
  Carrot Cake Smoothie, 197
  Mint Chocolate Chip Smoothie, 42
  Strawberry Banana Green Smoothie, 40
snow peas
  Tempeh and Snow Peas, 155
soba noodles, buckwheat
  Pad Thai Soba Noodles, 112
sorghum flour
  about, 12
  Cinnamon Pumpkin Donuts, 63
soups
  Brilliant Beet Soup, 174
  Carrot Rutabaga Butternut Bisque, 179

Cheesy Potato Soup, 180
Cream of Shiitake Soup, 176
Creamy Tomato Bisque, 80
Kabocha, Apple, and Fennel Bisque, 79
Super Easy Veggie Broth, 171
Sweet Potato Cauliflower Soup, 175
Zesty Black Bean Soup, 148
Spaghetti Squash with Broccoli and Button Mushrooms, 173
spinach
  Mint Chocolate Chip Smoothie, 42
  Spinach Artichoke Dip, 36
  Strawberry Banana Green Smoothie, 40
squash
  Carrot Rutabaga Butternut Bisque, 179
  Delicata Squash Millet Bowl, 183
  Half and Half Marinara Sauce, 198
  Kabocha, Apple, and Fennel Bisque, 79
  Rustic Ratatouille, 170
  Spaghetti Squash with Broccoli and Button Mushrooms, 173
Stealthy Healthy Mayo, 139
strawberries
  Kiwi Salad, 86
  Strawberry Banana Green Smoothie, 40
sugar, about, 13
Summertime Quinoa Bowl, 57
Sun-Dried Tomato Guacamole, 82
sunflower seeds
  Dried Fruit Salad, 87
  Get Up and Go Granola, 58
  Korean Napa Tacos, 22
Sunshine Breakfast UnScramble, 150
Super Easy Veggie Broth, 171
Superfresh Salsa, 83

supplements, 3
Sweet Mustard-Glazed Rapini, 35
sweet potatoes
  Cheesy Chili Sweet Potato Fries, 191
  Red Bean Sweet Potato Salad, 152
  Sweet Potato Cauliflower Soup, 175

T
Taco Salad, Serious, 19
teff flour
  Chocolate Brownie Cake, 69
  Chocolate Teff Waffles, 62
tempeh
  Curried Collard Wraps, 21
  Tempeh and Snow Peas, 155
Thai Peanut Dressing, 113
theobroma oil. See cacao butter
Three-Grain Breakfast Medley, 47
tofu, extra-firm
  Jicama and Beet Green Frittata, 196
  Popcorn Tofu, 145
  Sunshine Breakfast UnScramble, 150
tofu, silken
  about, 12
  Blueberries and Cream Mousse, 98
  Stealthy Healthy Mayo, 139
  White Bean Ranch Dressing, 161
tofu press, 15
tomatoes
  Beyond Good BBQ Sauce, 101
  Brilliant Beet Soup, 174
  Creamy Tomato Bisque, 80
  Half and Half Marinara Sauce, 198
  Light and Lemony Fusilli with Asparagus and Roasted Tomatoes, 72
  Orange Lentil Salad, 153
  Pizza Hummus, 158
  Roasted Corn and Cilantro Chili, 149

Rustic Ratatouille, 170

Summertime Quinoa Bowl, 57

Sun-Dried Tomato Guacamole, 82

Sunshine Breakfast UnScramble, 150

Super Easy Veggie Broth, 171

Superfresh Salsa, 83

Zucchini-Laced Fusilli, 167

Too Good for You to Be True Chocolate, 128

tools for cooking, 13–15, 63

V

vanilla

Chocolate-Covered Hemp Cookies, 124

Vanilla Almond Granola, 120

vinegar, apple cider

ACV Fizz, 105

W

wakame

Wakame Salad, 23

walnuts

Caramel Apple Parfaits, 96

Hunky Monkey Ice Cream, 97

Roasted Pears with Walnuts, 94

Walnut Arugula Pesto, 43

Walnut Eggplant Dip, 115

water, drinking, 5

watercress greens

Red Potato Watercress Salad, 28

watermelon

Minted Watermelon Salad, 85

White Bean Ranch Dressing, 161

White Chocolate Peanut Butter Fudge Bites, 130

Wild Rice Pilaf, 53

Y

Yukon-Stuffed Poblanos, 164

Z

Zesty Black Bean Soup, 148

zucchini

Rainbow Veggie Chili, 147

Summertime Quinoa Bowl, 57

Zucchini-Laced Fusilli, 167